CHARCUTIER. SALUMIERE. WURSTMEISTER.

ELIZABETH PEPIN SILVA

FRANCOIS PAUL-ARMAND VECCHIO

REVIEW

A culinary *cri de Coeur* by Silva and Vecchio that explores the history, process and prospective future of sausage making.

This book approaches sausage creation as both art and science. It begins by introducing readers to the industry's leading artisans from Spain, France, Italy and Switzerland, who each offer their unique philosophies regarding their trade. Despite their differences, however, all are bound by their dedication to making quality pork products. The author's study focuses on the care and attention that these artisanal producers bestow upon their work, culminating in a diary-style recounting of Hawaii-based Thomas Pickett experiences giving pork seminars. An in-depth examination of the current state of the sausage industry follows, which can be read as a call to arms. The authors ask for a reevaluation of the industry core values—namely, they advocate a return to quality over quantity. They also look at how traditional approaches not only make for a better tasting sausage, but are also more environmental sound.

The book heralds a new wave of chefs and butchers who have a respect for sustainability, humane husbandry, organic growth and ecology. It also offers a series of educational chapters that tackle important subjects such as spices, salting, chopping, stuffing, tying and aging. Alongside the fundamentals, the authors consider the minutiae of the craft, such as the role of activated proteins during the mixing process. They also include more than 40 detailed. Step-by-step recipes for everything from the ominous headcheese -- a sausage made from snout, lips, cheek and tongue – to the deliciously spicy nduja sausage from Calabria. This approacheable, elegant book, clearly the result of extensive research, will appeal to master butchers as well to ambitious cooks.

A study that may become the new sausage master's bible, outstanding in its range, depths and clarity.

indie@kirkusreview.com

INTRODUCTIONS

By ARI WEINZWEIG, founder and co-owner of ZINGERMAN'S in Ann Arbor, Michigan.

It's well over twenty years ago since I met Francois Vecchio for the first time. I'm sure it was at a Fancy Food Show, more likely than not in New York City. In a huge convention hall, overloaded with kitsch, crass, and flash, Francois was one of the few who stood out to me—a beacon of calm, considered, caring intelligence. It took only a few sample slices of his carefully crafted cured meats and a few minutes of talking about what made them so special for me to realize that he was a person of great passion and a skilled craftsman. A bit more talking and it was clear too that he, like me, was taken with tradition. He had, and has, a commitment to quality that went way beyond the superficial. While everyone talked about quality, Francois was actually explaining—in great detail—why his products tasted as good as they did. By the end of that first conversation, it was clear to me that the man was all about meat quality. The things other vendors at the show were so concerned about—market share, selling to the mainstream, making do with mediocre in order to keep price points low, weren't a part of his repertoire.

Paul Goodman, the great 20th century anarchist philosopher, poet and writer said that, "The persons who separate themselves from nature have to live every minute of their lives without the power, joy and freedom of nature." Conversely, he argued, "Merely by continuing to exist and act in nature and freedom, a man wins the victory, establishes the "free" society;' it is not necessary for him to be a victor *over* anyone. When he creates, he wins; when he corrects his prejudices and habits, he wins; when he resists and suffers, he wins." I doubt that Francois Vecchio ever knew, or even knew of, Paul Goodman but all of what he wrote could well have been about Francois. Where most others have long since wavered, Francois has remained, unwilling to give in to the pressure toorm, to compromise quality. He was then and is now, steadfast, committed to all that is true, natural, and right about traditional charcuterie.

For me, the study of and passion for traditionally cured meat was one I came to as an adult. For Francois it was a way of life, really, I think, the only one he's known. "On the Vecchio side," he said, "my granddad was born in the 'Piemonte', 'Le Langhe', and started a wholesale meat business in Geneva. On my mother's side my grandpa had the best restaurant in Geneva, Restaurant Chouard. He had learned the trade in London, Aswan, Davos and the Black Forest." To say that Francois is a man of the world might be an under statement. He's been a butcher's apprentice in Switzerland, France, and

Italy. As a young man he spent time as shepherd in Colorado. He's made charcuterie in Switzerland and then, long before good food was where it is today, in 1981, he started to make traditional salami out in the Central Valley, California.

One of the things I loved about Francois from the first day I met him was his energy—calm, considered, almost stately but still down to earth and at the same time, intelligent and insightful. His passion is always present, but he's not a TV Food Network personality. You have to be willing to really listen, to care deeply, to tap into and appreciate his enthusiasm. But once you tap it, you realize that you've come upon one of the wise men of the food world. I feel so fortunate to have stayed with our initial food show conversation long enough to realize who and what I'd come across. Because I was the student, in this case in the world of traditional pork, Francois became my professor. Whatever it was that I wanted to know about salami, about ham curing, salting, smoking, etc. Francois was—and is—my go to guy. Over the years he has patiently talked me through science I could barely understand, told me tales of Saucisson de Lyon, regaled me with the lovely history of Rosette de Lyon, and shared the "secrets" of Swiss salami. He's waxed poetic about prosciutto, shared stories of old school air curing, expounded on the whys and hows of the perfect pork fat, and marveled at the seemingly miraculous, but still scientifically sound workings of the molds and bacteria that make all these cured meats what they are.

All of which is conveyed, carefully, thoughtfully, and clearly in the book you're holding in your hands. For me, getting to read Francois' work was far more exciting than any big headline, social media or high society award ceremony. While most of what's out there tends towards the superficial, Francois and his work are all about substance. Which is, of course, the way it's been for his whole life. Where everyone else was all about marketing slogans, Francois was working to teach American hog farmers how to raise animals with meat good enough to make great charcuterie here in the US. Where others were working over new fad diets, Francois was appreciating the subtleties of flavor, the nuance and nicety that most people, even most professionals, never notice. Salami, the way I learned it from Francois, was at a whole new level, an entirely new eating experience, radically different from what I'd known previously. Never, ever, ever he taught me, should you have those all too typical strings stuck between your teeth or that oh so unpleasant heartburn half an hour after you ate. He taught me to tell the difference between the mediocre mass-market salami (flat tasting, one dimensional, greasy, stringy and heartburn provoking) and what a great, world-class traditional "salame" could be—aromatic, beautifully perfumed, complex, long lingering.

When I wrote the chapter on salami in Zingerman's Guide to Good Eating, Francois was my muse. The master that I felt fortunate to be able to sit, so to speak, by the slicer to learn from. The contrast between Francois and everyone else I spoke to was significant. Speaking of which, while everyone else was talking about SKUs in supermarkets, Francois was patiently explaining why salami didn't just need to be made well, it needed to be handled perfectly. That it should never be sliced more than minutes—hours at the most—before it was going to be eaten to avoid unnecessary oxidation. How slicing it at the wrong angle, too thick or too thin, pressing on the slicer so hard that the fat was being forced out of the meat, would all detract from the eating experience.

The care and consideration Francois has always given to cured meat—expressed insightfully in this book as it has been in all our conversations over the years—is very much what one would now expect from the world class coffee roaster or the award winning barista. While the rest of the world is making and drinking mediocre espresso every day, the best espresso is a revelation. Every detail—from bean selection to roasting to freshness to the slightest variation in grind to the exactitude of the water temperature and bars of pressure on the machine and the number of seconds it takes to pull the shot are in play. The best of the best—and I try to frequent them regularly, will ooh and ah (as well they ought) when the "crema" comes out just right, talk about the spice notes and hints of fruit. They call out the finish, the nose and the niceties of the texture.

With espresso, as we enter the middle of the second decade of the 21st century, those sorts of conversations have become quite common.

Francois Vecchio has been having comparable conversations about "salame" for most of his life. The same attention to detail, the poetry, the passion, knowing how much every tiny shift in production will impact the flavor, texture and aroma of the finished product are what he's always been fascinated about. "Scientifically," he says, "you can never describe quality." He generously lumps himself in with the rest of us when he says, "We forgot that food is for the senses. It's a shame." Francois's amazing energy, the excellence of everything he makes, and in this case, his book, works because he himself is fully congruent with what he is crafting. Everything about him and his work conveys quality. He brings the scientific finesse of a physicist, the professionalism and passion of a Pablo Casals, the palate and expertise of Alice Waters to his work. All of which is detailed in the book you hold in your hands.

I can't quite decide if Francois is ahead of, or of an era that's long since, sadly, passed. But really, I guess the answer is both. For anyone who cares about traditional food, as I have for so long, what Francois has to say, the quality of his work and his life, are actually timeless. Francois and his cured meats are what great food has always been about. And, trends and TV shows be damned, they are what it will *always* be about for as long as good people care about eating good food. I look forward to many more years of all of that and I'm happy to know that many others in the world will now get to meet the man who's played such a positive role in teaching what really good charcuterie is all about.

All that said, neither Francois, nor any of us, will live forever. But by taking the time to put together this book, filled as it is with amazing anecdotes, history, the details and nuance that go into properly and traditionally curing great pork, the sense of history and passion and pretty much everything to do with beautifully cured pork products is here. I don't think I'm being overly negative to say that Francois has never gotten the recognition from the food world that I believe he deserves. And yet, I believe his passion, knowledge, wisdom and skill are a wonderful gift we have been given. It's an honor to hold this book in my hands, a distillation of Francois' many years of study, skill and devotion to sensory subtlety and of course, great salami. I cherish it as I cherish all the time that I've had to learn, study and taste with the master.

Ari Weinzweig is co-founding partner of Zingerman's Community of Businesses in Ann Arbor, Michigan. Ari was recognized as one of the "Who's Who of Food & Beverage in America" by the 2006 James Beard Foundation and was awarded a Bon Appetit Lifetime Achievement Award among many recognitions. Ari is the author of a number of articles and books, including "Zingerman's Guide to Better Bacon" (Zingerman's Press), "Zingerman's Guide to Giving Great Service" (Hyperion), "Zingerman's Guide to Good Eating" (Houghton Mifflin), and "Zingerman's Guide to Good Leading, Part 1: A Lapsed Anarchist's Approach to Building a Great Business." His most recent book is "Zingerman's Guide to Good Leading, Part 2: A Lapsed Anarchist's Approach to Being a Better Leader." He is currently at work on his next book, "Zingerman's Guide to Good Leading, Part 3; A Lapsed Anarchist's Approach to Managing Ourselves."

By CHRISTOPHER LEE, consulting chef and owner of Pop-Up General Store in Berkeley, California.

As "salumieri", we stand in the European tradition. Apart from the remarkable, and sometimes exquisite country hams and smoked bacon of the South, we in the U.S. do not possess an indigenous tradition of "salumi". Our tradition springs from a Western European one brought here by immigrants who settled some of our large Eastern cities, and our practices and products are mostly French, Italian, Spanish, and German. This what has defined our sensibilities about meat curing and has determined our tastes for cured meats; it is that tradition we emulate in the sausage kitchen.

As a student of "salumi", how does one learn the techniques and grasp the necessary understanding that inform our curing room practices? It typically means years of travel and working abroad to study and understand the fundamental and essential skills of our craft. Absent that experience, we improvise and imagine what is in fact the long, respected, and comprehensible history and practice of "salumi" and charcuterie. Such experiments are not consistently successful.

When I started curing meats 20 years ago (like many, as a complete and utter novice) I had the incredible luck of meeting François Vecchio, then master artisan "salumiere" at Columbus Salame Company in San Francisco. I'd come across a terrific article on Tuscan "salumieri" that traced exactly the path I'd taken in previous years through the Chianti Valley to work with several local producers. The article detailed the author's sojourn in Gaiole, Radda, and Greve, and the incredible "salumi" that he encountered there, made from both "Cinta Senese", the Tuscan pig, and from the wild boar that roam the Tuscan hillsides. I was excited to think that these products would be available in the U.S. Near the end of the article came the deathblow; they could not be imported into the U.S. because of USDA regulations.

I was encouraged when the author mentioned that one could find equally special meats here, made with the same care and understanding as their European counterparts by François Vecchio; the master "salumiere" was making these meats just across the Bay. I immediately called Columbus and asked if I could speak to him. The person who gruffly answered the call went to fetch François. When François took the phone, I politely introduced myself and explained how I had found him and what I'd been doing. Then, with what I came to understand is his usual generosity and graciousness, François said to come see him.

Later on, he offered to visit me at the restaurant, and was soon demonstrating, describing, and passing on his incomparable knowledge freely in his typical teacher-like manner. He asked nothing in return for this information. Well, perhaps he took an occasional meal in the kitchen, but nothing more. I remember when I showed him some of the early salami I'd made that I had been relatively satisfied with, he said it was a good start, but quite "casalinga"-- homemade looking and tasting, and with faults. Over time he showed me what I needed to do to make "more professional salami." Immediately things began to change in the curing shed.

It was a fortuitous discovery for me. François already had a long history of meat curing from his native Switzerland when he came to the U.S. to make California's tastiest "salumi". I didn't yet know his name when in the mid-1980's I tasted the fine, European-style "salumi" from Rapelli, which I later learned was François's salami company. Here in the U.S., François Vecchio is our link to that tradition, and perhaps our sole source of that history, tradition, and technique. He seems to know everything about "salumi", "charcuterie", and "Wurst", and no matter how arcane the question I bring to him, he has not just an answer, but *the* answer. It's remarkable, and never ceases to amaze me.

I've been lucky to continue my study with François, and to continue to learn from him over nearly 20 years how to think about "salumi"; how to improve it; how to "keep the little bugs happy" that help transform the meat through fermentation and drying into a proper, delicious, cured product; and to use my hands and nose to assess quality. A young friend of mine likens meat curing to alchemy, though I can't say with certainty that it contains elements of religion, mythology, and spirituality. But maybe it does. Another budding "salumiere" described François as our Obi-Wan Kenobi, and with that I can agree.

It is because of François's work and teaching that we see the enthusiastic discovery everywhere of the craft of "salumi" making. It is on the minds and in the hands of many chefs and butchers these days. I ran into some great "salumi" quite unexpectedly on a recent trip through Virginia and North Carolina, and it was of excellent quality.

Nearly every day I think about François and his influence – he's vital, healthy, and an inspiration to all us "salumiere" – and worry that we'll miss the opportunity to preserve what he knows. I do not have to wonder where "salumi" in the U.S. would be without him. I hope we are wise enough to embrace and conserve his knowledge for the future, and pass it on to those who follow behind. Certainly his book will help to achieve that needed and important task.

Christopher Lee went to university in the Midwest, and later turned his career to cooking, leading to 16 years with Alice Waters' renowned Chez Panisse Restaurant in Berkeley, California. Afterward he opened his own Italian restaurant, Eccolo, also in Berkeley, and since 2009 has been consulting in the U.S. and Europe. He is passionately involved in gourmet "charcuterie" and "salumi".

CHARCUTIER. SALUMIERE. WURSTMEISTER

European Tradition for Quality

Why such a book?

In "C'est une Chose Etrange à la Fin que le Monde" Jean d'Ormesson, the French philosopher and member of the "Académie Française", points to two ways of human nature to relate to the World :

> … When they discover, one after the other, the hidden laws of nature and what they call **reality**, they are doing **Science**.

> … When they yield to their imagination and create what they call **beauty**, they are doing **Art**.

Science, product of the thinking mind, can create reflected descriptions and images of the world. It is the domain of numbers and technology, the reign of **Quantity**.

Art, the domain of the soul, uses sensitivity, intuition, and the experiencing of life. It reigns over **Beauty** and **Quality**. It is the realm of **Skill and Craft**.

One cannot describe the other. Both art and science are complementary human functions. They demand to balance in life, **Quantity** and **Quality**.

In this book

- First, we will take a tour of friends who are the artisans, the "Salchichoner", "Charcutier", and "Salumiere", expressing the skills and craft, each in their unique situation, in Cataluña, France, Switzerland, and Italy. This way we will get an idea of what we will explore in this book.

- Second, we read a humorous view from a participant in one seminar in Palmer, AK.

- Third, we take a look at the world of meat as it is today and what is missing.

- Fourth, in the context of the European tradition, we examine all the steps of the production aiming at quality.

- Fifth, we propose recipes for the use of the whole animal and cover all the different techniques.

- Sixth, we discuss the art of fermenting, drying and aging including information about the starter cultures.

Complementing this book is an 82 minute professional DVD movie by Liz Pepin Silva, edited by Kirk Goldberg.

THE ART AND PHILOSOPHY OF PRODUCING QUALITY PORK PRODUCTS

In this movie, François Vecchio, knife in hand, demonstrates how to break, bone and trim a carcass to be able to select each muscle and fat type, according to their ability to be used in the proper type of recipe. In an introduction and all along the demonstration, François discusses all the aspects, which are critical to the craft.

The DVD movie is published by CreateSpace a division of Amazon and is available at http://www.amazon.com. The author strongly recommends to peruse both DVD and book to gain a full sharing of his experience.

In his Internet website http://www.francoisvecchio.com/breaking-and-trimming-the-whole-pig/, a power-point presentation in four sections: Break, Shoulder, Middle and Leg, is available.

Each professional picture by Elizabeth Pepin Silva shows step-by-step how François breaks, bones and trims the carcass.

CONTENTS

ARTISANS

of
Spain, France, Italy and Switzerland

SALCHICHONER
CHARCUTIER or "GRATTE-LARD"
SALUMIERE

Cataluña, Lyon, Ticino, Romagna, Bassa Parmense, Alps

Ten Artisans at Work in Different Traditions of Southern Europe

June 2010

SPAIN, CATALUNA, GARROTXA, OLOT, TURON
MAGI SALA

Magi is a unique treasure. He is a scientist with degrees in microbiology and biochemistry who is practicing the old tradition of the "salchichoner" in the Valley of the Garrotxa high in the Catalan mountains.

After years of travel, he lives today in Olot and manages, again, a big plant which he helped design in the late 80's. He has crossed the world to consult and advise within the industry to create and improve numerous products. He is, to my knowledge the only scientist with an intimate knowledge of the meat and is able to hold a knife and make his own sausages.

All those wonderful changes that we observe in the processes from raw meat to mature products have no secrets from him and, still, he relates to the craft, not by an abstract, quantified sum of knowledge but by the direct apprehension and experiencing of quality as any traditional old hand.

"Back-slopping" to improve the activity of the fermenting

Better than the old "back-slopping" process for starter inoculation, Magi ferments for 5 days at 15°C, a pre-batch inoculated with starters, which is incorporated to the new batch of meat. The result is better, faster fermentation and an improved product.

SPAIN, CATALUNA, VIC, CASA SANDRA
PABLO ARBOIX PUJOL

Pablo is an esthete, the master of the **"salchichon de Vich"**, noblest of all sausages in Spain.

He lives by his commandments:
1. Never buy meat from the trade.
2. Use the whole and sort and trim by hand.
3. Let nature play.

His plant was built in 1908 in a location, which today has become the heart of the ancient city of Vic. Across the street, his shop features the "Salchichon" in a décor befitting the best gems.

"En todas las artes, y esto tambien incluye el arte del buen comer, el gran rafinamiento consiste en la sintesis y la simplicidad.

Evidentemente es necessario hacer referencia a la tradition, para no traicionarla por ignorancia, por negligencia o per omission.

Asi es como perduramos, que en la elaboracion de un product. Reconocemos solamente la ley del equilibrio impuesta por la naturaleza".

(In all the arts, and it includes the art of good eating, perfection is made of synthesis and simplicity.

It is evidently necessary to refer to tradition, to not betray it by ignorance, neglect or omission.

This is how we endure in the elaboration of a product. We recognize uniquely the law of balance, imposed by nature).

Salchichoner's jewels showcase.

Best in Spain.

FRANCE, LYON, CAPITAL OF THE GAULS
JEAN PLASSE

Jean Plasse,

Jean is the son and grandson of "Charcutier du Beaujolais". His life is dedicated to the art of good food and good wine, "Chevalier" or "Grand Maître" of the Guilds protecting the crafts of Lyon.

A "bon vivant" with a passion for good, he is still running fast at 75. We met in the "Halles de Lyon" to visit with the best and share a memorable repast.

"Jésus, saucissons and rosettes".   The best name in "Les Halles".

Saucissons pistachés à cuire.

Jean's daughter, **Chantal Plasse,** maintains the tradition of the "saucisson" produced in her kitchen of Jassans, on the Saone, upstream from Lyon. There, she also regroups the finest charcuteries, selected from all the local traditions of France and services 10 shops from Nice to Berlin, which she operates under the name of the family cradle "La Ferme Beaujolaise", like embassies of the French "bien manger".

She is also quite well known in the United States as a supplier of "Fromages affinés de France" and hoping one day to be able to supply "saucisson aux truffes, pistaches" and other "sabaudet" to American gourmets.

Chantal Plasse with her friend Gérard Lobietti, owner of Gast.

"Saucisson à cuire et saucisson pistaché".

In Jassans, near Villefranche on the river Saone, we cooked and cut the saucisson.

Cutter, blender, and stuffer are the tools of the trade.

The coarse ground paste is stuffed in large beef casings and then hung to dry in a room at 50 to 60°F for a few days. It is enough to cure the meat and get a very light fermentation, which sets the meat.

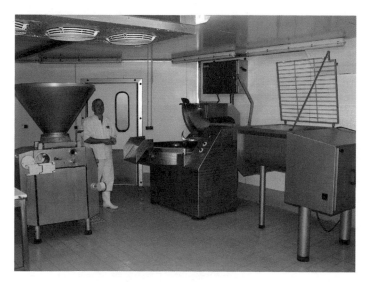

Stuffer, cutter and blender.

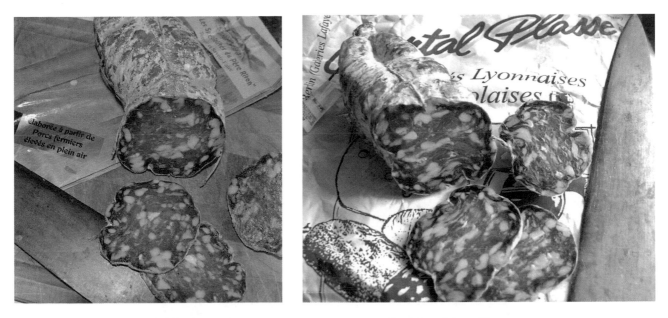

Classic French "saucisson sec", stuffed in chitterling.

A full case of exceptional goodies at "La Ferme Beaujolaise".

"Les pâtés en croûte de Chantal".

"Les crus", all the dry cured varieties.

… not only does it take knowledge, but heart and a fine mouth…

Monsieur George Reynon

FRANCE, OLD CITY OF LYON
GEORGE REYNON

George is a praised master of the craft in the old City. He runs the family business in "la rue des Archers" making anything that the art of "charcutier and traiteur" allows in the tradition of Lyon. His pride is in the maturing of the finest "rosette, jésus" and "saucisson de Lyon".

In the narrow streets of Old Lyon, between Rhône and Saone, Monsieur Reynon cuddles his "rosette" and "saucisson de Lyon".

A store of great reputation, rue des Archers.

The unique "saucisson de Lyon" is unctuous and mellow.
The secret is a paste worked with leaf lard to stay soft after fermenting and aging.

Monsieur Reynon in front of his drying room.
All the "saucissons" are perfectly shaped.

SWITZERLAND, TICINO, MAROGGIA
KELLER FAMILY

The Keller Family operates a jewel of a little plant not too far from Lugano on the shore of a beautiful lake. Though their name sounds German, they are real "ticinesi" and have been there for a long time.

They are very proud of the high quality of their products which include all the typical products enjoyed in this part of the world; amongst these the "salametti" are prominent. They come in two types "nostrano", coarse ground or "Milano", fine ground.

The meat, all pork, is hand trimmed and processed on the classic Italian line made by Velati in Milano. The paste is rested for 1-2 days to cure and bind, then stuffed in pork middle casing and hand-tied in chains of little links - about 3" long.

The phase of fermenting and drying lasts one whole week at a relatively low initial temperature of 20°C, followed by a short aging time during which an abundant mold is grown. The goal is to ship a still soft, very fragrant, sweet and mellow "salametti" at 25% of shrinkage with hardly any acidification.

Velati grinder, salt dispenser, conveyor, "spargitrice"(spreader) and mixer.

Toward the end of the fermenting and drying phase, the "salametti" start to grow some mold.

The "salametti" age in a room, where the wood has been preserved to harbor the traditional flora and maintain the aroma.

Note the heat coils on the floor and the static cold coil on the ceiling, with the gutter collecting the condensed water; this setting provides a very gentle natural flow of the air to avoid any crusting of the salami.

SWITZERLAND, TICINO, CASTEL SAN PIETRO, SALUMEIRA ARTIGIANALE

At the foot of Monte Generoso on the southern tip of Switzerland, I found a small "macelleria" where the master and two "macellai" were stuffing, binding, and netting "mortadella di fegato".

"Salametti, mortadelle di fegato, salame Milano, salame nostrano" in the village boutique.

Ancient horizontal stuffer.

Antique grinder.

Masterful hands.

"Mortadella di fegato" is made with softer meats, fat and some liver. It is stuffed in a pork casing and slightly dried, usually cooked for consuming as a cold cut, which has some similarity with the French "pâté de campagne", but it has much more of an enticing flavor due to the slight fermenting during the drying phase. The locals eat it raw like salami. The texture stays soft and the aroma is very rich.

SWITZERLAND, TICINO, CASTEL SAN PIETRO
CAPOFERRI FAMILY
SALUMIFICIO DEL MONTE

Father, twin sons Sandro and Enzo and daughter run a small plant where quality is reigning supreme.

Their prosciutto is one of the best prosciutto I have ever tasted. They select the legs, one by one from the best Swiss pork.

Salting.

Papa Capoferri in front of the legs washed after the salt.

Right, salt crusted after "riposo". Left, after washing, ready for "asciugamento" (drying and fermenting).

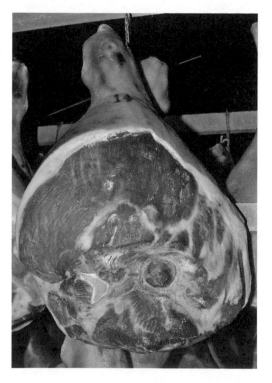

Ready for drying after "asciugamento".

Drying racks.

Aging after "stuccagio" (spreading with lard, mixed
with salt and pepper, which stops the drying).

Aging "prosciutto stuccato".

During all the sequences of the process, care has been taken to avoid any crusting or cracking. The leg is still perfectly shaped and homogeneous for the final aging, which will last up to 18 months.

In Ticino they also like chorizo.

"Pancette piane". Note that the rib meat is left on.

Shaping the "fidighella" or "mortadella di fegato".

Tasting the goodies, "salame tipo nostrano".

ITALY, EMILIA ROMAGNA, ALFONSINE
DANIELE ALBERANI

Daniele with "pancetta arrotolata".   Papa Alberani.

Daniele operates with his father a specialized plant in Alfonsine, near Ravenna in the heart of the rich Romagna. They salt, cure, dry and age in the way of the local tradition "coppa, lonzo, pancetta" in different shapes and forms and a very special prosciutto which is processed boned and trimmed. This is a new development in Italy, which supplements the ancient "culatello" and "speck Tirolese", with "culaccia, fiocco" and other variations of the leg trim.

They are very careful to select the best meats available, in quality and also in the way they are trimmed and prepared, dry curing with sea salt, slow fermenting and drying, followed by a long aging.

The place is remarkable for its creativity in expanding from the sheer tradition with products which offer conveneience for the food services. They ship througout Italy all the way to Sicily.

"Pancette piane stagionate".

"Coppe stagionate".

The boneless prosciutto.

The production process is similar to the classic Italian prosciutti but starts with a carefully trimmed boneless leg. The art resides in a very gentle handling in order to avoid any crusting of the meat, which will result in cracks, impossible to close.

Except for the salting done on shelves, the meat is constantly hanging.

ITALY, SAN BIAGIO DI ARGENTA, FERRARA
MAURO MALAFONTE

Following in the step of his father, Mauro started 8 years ago "NATURAL SALAMI". The shop is dedicated only to salame, the best of the best. The plant is small with less than 10 employees and he only sells locally.

Daniele Alberani, friend and collegue, helped to get him started.

Mauro, a real artist, pays a lot of attention to the origin of the meat and the way it is trimmed and prepared. His pride are the salami made with the whole meat of "La Mora" pigs, which are produced in an ancient way, free to forage outside, in the farms of the Appenini.

They are an old local breed of black pigs roaming freely, growing slowly, and fattened in the fall on acorn and chestnut. Their carcasses at 18 months, when they are deemed mature, are heavy, reaching 400 lb.

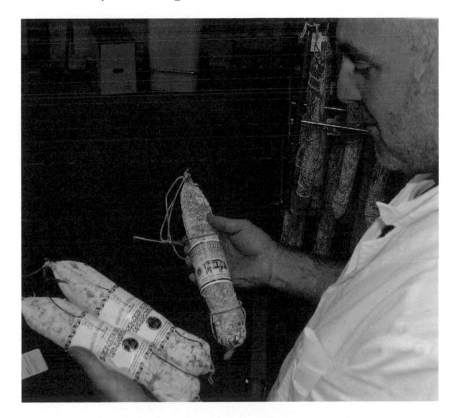

Meat of the Mora pork, salt, sugar, pepper (all organic);
some of the best I've ever tasted!

Daniele and his friend Mauro.

He makes these special Salami, with the whole carcass of "La Mora.

Mauro hold two of his "Salame della Mora" and a unique "Salame della Mora, organico", which he lovingly ages for months.

Stuffing il "budello gentile".   Tying.

The second day during the drying phase, the salami has fermented, changed color, and firmed up, but the casing is still soft and permeable.

Salami after four days in "asciugamento";
the mold starts on the casing.

Mauro and his "salame in budello gentile".

Everything he makes is coarse ground in the local tradition. He uses no ingredients other than sea salt, nitrate, and pepper. No starter cultures, the environment and the origin and quality of the meats provide for it. Low acidity, slow fermentation and patient aging, deliver the expected rich and delicate aroma of his salami.

ITALY, LA FATTORIA DI PARMA
PAOLO PONGOLINI

The low and foggy Plain of "La Bassa Parmense" between Parma and the river Po, is the home of the "culatello". By many considered the absolute best of the many types and form of the Italian prosciutto.

In Sanguinaro on the Via Emilia, there is a beautiful store, which is famous for "culatello". It attracts many visitors who come from all over the World.

Paolo runs the place following in the steps of his ancestors. The picture of "San Antonio" traditionally, was hanging over the gate of the ancient barn and presided over the celebration of the pig slaughter at the farm in the thick of winter. That is when his grandfather started the business, passing on the tradition. Paolo uses this same picture of "San Antonio, "protettore dei porcelli" on his label.

Paolo is very focused, fixed on quality and tradition. He makes only the products of the local tradition, very proud of showing his products. He took me to an aging room set to accommodate visitors and customers for presentation and demonstration of his specialties. The tasting of an 18 month old "culatello", anyway, tells me more than a long description.

"Paolo Pongolini nel negozio".

Fragrant and beautiful "culatello" to temp the visitor.

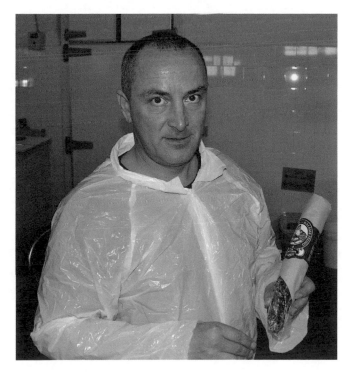

Paolo holds a "salame felino".

"Lo strolghino, famoso dolce e fragrante".

Attractively packaged "culatelli" and, below, quartered "prosciutti".

Before serving, the aged "culatello" has to soak in white wine. Beside the addition of the wine bouquet, it softens the exposed muscle, which has hardened during the aging months.

"Culaccia, noce, fiocco, prosciutto and culatello".

"Culatelli" in the aging room.

ITALY, VALLE D'OSSOLA, MASERA, IL DIVIN PORCELLO
MASSIMO SARTORETTI

In the deep valley of Ossola, which leads to the Simplon pass is an old village, built of the gneiss and granite of the mountains, some centuries ago by sturdy peasants,

Massimo Sartoretti maintains the family tradition. He has transformed old barns into a delicious and elegant hostel, which is well known all the way to Milan.

Gourmets come here to enjoy the fabulous "salumi" that his father, still running strong at 70, produces in his shop installed in a 300 years old stone farm.

Warden of tradition.

Hostel of the divine porker.

Antipasto of "mortadella di fegato", rye bread with walnuts, "prosciutto, coppa, guanciale, salame nostrano, carne secca, lonzo, pancetta piana"… The taste of the fat is incredibly delicious.

Classic prosciutto slicer.

Masera.

This old door was once the gate to the sheep barn. Papa Sartoretti
takes me to his aging rooms.

Charcutier. Salumiere. Wurstmeister.

"Violini di capra" amongst the "prosciutti".

"Stagionatura in cantina".

"Prosciutti" rest after salting and legs in salt. 30 varieties of herbs, color the curing salt.

Now that we have toured old Europe, we have a feeling for the tradition. We get a sense of what defines QUALITY. We may even have our mouth watering at some pictures... I wish we could take the tour together, but we need to come back and look at what is happening here in the good, ole USA. As a very good example, listen to Thomas Pickett, owner of The Kilauea Bakery and Pau Hana Pizza on Kaua'i, Hawai'i. He is an amazing fellow, a genius of a kind. He spent a week in Palmer, Alaska attending one of our seminars and workshops. On a later visit to his bakery in Hawai'i, he surprised me with a creation of his own. I had never seen or tasted anything like it before: a black bratwurst... I will have to remember to ask him for the recipe!
He handles the pen even better than his knife. Enjoy his narrative of the seminar in Palmer

---

THE PIG GIG
THOMAS PICKETT, Baker in Kilauea, Kaua'i, Hawai'i.
BY NOW, A "CHARCUTIER" AND OCCASIONAL WRITER. HE RELATES HIS EXPERIENCES AS A PORK SEMINARIST.

Monday April 15, 2013
I thought it was humorous that six strangers sit down together in a dinner banquet at a remote inn on the outskirts of Anchorage, Alaska and five of them had photographs of pigs or pork as favorite shots on smart phones.

Tuesday April 16, 2012
It took two of us to lift the carcass off the hook and lay on the table. The scent of it hung in the air of the butcher shop despite the wall-to-wall antiseptic wash from the night before. We tested the blades of our knives. Stephan Silva, an adroit chef with a fondness for quality, ran his thumb over a blade of laminated VG-10 "super steel". Jason Jillson, originally Stephan's chef de cuisine but recently turned free agent in the culinary theater of San Francisco, casually opened his tool kit to select a well-used boning knife.

Ruby Duke from Raven and Boar Farm in New York ran a critical eye over the meat on the table and compared the slaughter marks to her own work. It was obvious even to me that the meat had been roughly handled. The head had been lopped off with the entire jowl attached. The knife thrust to the jugular, a bit too enthusiastically, had ruined some of the Boston Butt. Someone explained that in these parts prisoners of the local Federal penitentiary slaughter the pigs in a work program. I wasn't sure how to feel about that. Couldn't we teach them knitting?

Ruby was running on just a few hours of sleep after flying thousands of miles to the territory of Alaska to spend a week with four men in a butcher shop. She called it a vacation. I was in the company of some high functioning foodies. We had come from the far corners of the empire to participate in a six-day workshop on the craft of cutting and preparing cured pork products. Italians call it "salumi", the French, "charcuterie".

I picked up my old knife and shaved a few hairs off my forearm. I knew Francois, our teacher, would politely discard it as a baker's knife, a baker long out of circulation in the world of fine food. "Salame" for me stubbornly remained something you get in the supermarket in vacuum-sealed plastic and spelled with an "i". I didn't discriminate between varieties as long as there had been no recent news of salmonella poisoning. My knowledge of "salame" could be summed up in three thoughts: It came in large or small circles, you ate it on sandwiches and once you opened the package and peeled off a few slices you put it back in the fridge where it may never be heard from again.

Our first demonstration began. François spoke quietly, "Shall we start then?" He lifted the back leg of the pig and began cutting. His movements were confident and measured. He described every cut, every bone and muscle. I was watching someone so comfortable in their work it could be done blind folded. The blade moved as if it was part of his hand. He used muscle memory and experience to find his way and the pieces deftly separated into ham, loin, CT butt and ribs. This was knife handling by a master.

François is a handsome Swiss gentleman who began his career long ago as teenage apprentice in a Paris butcher shop. He has spent decades perfecting his art and working into the upper echelon of the industry. His career spans a major transformation of how our population feeds itself. Where we now derive most of our sustenance from a huge automated food industry he remembers when people grew and prepared foods more regionally, closer to home.

We are gathered here in the Matanuska-Susitna Valley of Alaska to see and learn from a master "salumiere", a sausage maker of the highest regard. Little did we know we would also be infused with François' passion for the more logical process of a small village economy and his disdain for the monstrous industry he had witnessed his art mutate to.

As the pig was transformed into clean cuts of meat and neat piles of useful bone and skin François' narration of his demo was peppered with warm and humorous stories from a past when a cured ham or stick of "salame" had a crop, a farm and a local sausage maker connected to it. Being Swiss François speaks his native tongue and the languages of most of Switzerland's four neighbors, sometimes all in one sentence. Today I listened to him begin a story in English then casually slip between Swiss, French, Italian and finally finishing in that melting pot called English. Although I'm just semi-literate in only one language I felt poly-lingual there for a moment. He described how a butcher, can literally feel the difference in quality between the flesh of a pig that was raised on a farm by a caring family and one that was treated as a commodity.

After hours of detailed knife work and explanation François needed a break. His lovely wife Christine laid out a spread of fresh fruit and vegetables. We brought several recently crafted sticks of salami and cured meat to a cutting board. I was still trying to develop a fondness for salami. Of course I love bratwurst sizzling on the grill. And who can pass up breakfast sausage or bacon on a Sunday morning, but eight kinds of dried salami? Francois and Stephan kept talking about something called "nostrano". To me, that sounded like a Sicilian crime family.

But then François reached and sliced off a paper-thin piece. He lifted the slice to his nose and smiled. He said, "Look at it, look at the particles inside and the clear delineation between the lean meat and the fat, smell the pleasantly mild, acidic aroma." He put it down and picked up the whole sausage. He gave the cut end a squeeze and pointed out the firmness, the color and the way no moisture nor melted fat appeared. Put that way I began to think I might learn to like it after all. I was definitely ready to try some now that it had been described in such a cultured way.

I gave in and tasted all eight along with three varieties of cured ham. By the end of lunch I was sure of two things; I had a new appreciation for artisanal salami and I would be requiring a renal regulator to balance the recent influx of salt into my system. A few pints of Alaskan artisanal beer might do the trick.

Wednesday April 17, 2012

I don't often take aspirin but when I do I eat three. Is Alaskan beer stronger than those in the lower 48? It might be the altitude, or maybe the latitude. Regardless of the after effects from the Midnight Sun Brewery, work in the shop began on time. After all we have plenty to do this week. The five of us are to transform four mature hogs into an exciting collection of "salumi". The list includes "atriaux, boudin noir, rillettes, pâté de champagne", headcheese, "mousse de foie", frankfurter, "saucisson de Lyon, cotechino, salame nostrano, sopressata, chorizo, jambon royal, speck Tirolese, lonzo, coppa" and several whole loin "porchetta" roasts. Once we finish we will serve many of them at a grand banquet for fifty hosted by the proprietor of Palmer Alaska's finest and most progressive restaurant, Turkey Red.

We began work today at 9am, a late start for a baker. There seems to be no rush to begin work up here because the days are so long. The sun comes up at a very casual pace, lighting up the sky long before it breaks over the mountain. It crosses overhead by the lengthiest possible route and then takes it's gay ol' time deciding to go back down. It's almost indecisive. I watched it set yesterday and it seemed to hang just above the horizon for hours.

Today our task was to break down a side of pork using Francois' example of the day before. We entered the back door of the shop to find Nate, the proprietor and host of our venue just finishing his morning work. Nate is a muscular man of average height with a wry smile and few words. His bread and butter, or steak and chops as it were are processing game animals for local hunters. Guys in florescent orange hunting vests, dirty pants and crazy hair drive up to his back door in dusty pickups or ATV's. Lying in the back are examples of subsistence living, Alaskan style. Moose, elk, bear and other game feed the folks well up here. How well? I dare you to put "wagyu" beef up against the flavor and texture of a steak of Moose Tenderloin. Your average adult Moose weighs in at well over a thousand pounds. Nate and a small crew of seasonal butchers, often graduates of the state penitentiary, cut over 150,000 pounds of Moose during the summer and fall hunting season.

This morning a local farmer dropped off the family pig for processing. It hung on the hooks in very poor condition. Nate, succinctly, let us know his thoughts: Killed in the spring instead of the fall it was very lean. The slaughter technique was beyond bad. It looked like it had been tied to the back of a truck and dragged on the highway to skin it. This pig was an example of why Nate was hosting our workshop. He agreed with

François, we needed to recapture the quality of a civilization that loves and respects it's food. A barbarian had handled this unfortunate animal.

But that didn't stop Nate from doing his best. His job was to make the finished product look as good as possible and earn a living wage. After all profit is not a four-letter word, Loss is. The hog hung on the overhead rail by two hooks, one in the tendon of each rear hoof. Nate stood on the cement in front of it. He wore work boots and a butcher's apron over his t-shirt and jeans. Hanging at his right hip was a flat holster with a small utility grade boning knife, a larger blade and a honing steel. His bone saw was hanging off one hoof. A foot away was his band saw and at the end of it was a cutting table and bins for sorting the cuts. I wanted to film a production butcher at work so he waited a moment while I prepared. I held the camera up, he said, "Ready?" and drew his knife.

It was carcass to chops in twelve minutes, a blur of blades and flesh. Boning knife to sacrum, down through the hip, a bit of a saw work and the right hindquarter fell away. He hits the switch on the band saw and it whines to life. Right hindquarter to saw, slice and the hoof goes in the can, slice and the hock hits the bin, slice the shank hit's the bin and the rest is cut into ham and bone. Boning knife to left rear quarter and abdomen falls to the saw. One cut down the spine and then each side is cut rhythmically into short ribs, spare ribs, chops, tenderloin, and what was left of the belly became bacon. I was inspired. I walked into the inner kitchen to break my own hog.

Mine was just one side of a healthy specimen when I started. It took me three hours to finish and by the time I was done it was evident who in the room was the barbarian. Francois walked up to me at one point and in an affable way made a mincing motion toward my work with his hands and said, "Here it looks as if little rats have been chewing!"

Thursday April 18, 2012
The heads brine cured over night. We deboned them first thing this morning. Each of us started the day with a blank stare from Miss Piggy. Her gaze from the cutting board was pale and vacant. Francois started first. He casually flensed the entire mass of soft tissue from the skull in a single unfolded unit. Not one to be intimidated by fifty years of experience I began hacking away in my own primitive style. We put the bones and scraps into a pot with a few vegetables and aromatic herbs to simmer. It will eventually render a ridiculously rich stock. Both the meat and stock will be used in our Headcheese and a Bolognese sauce for one of our kitchen lunches.

Later we moved on to mixing and filling sausage casings with "salame nostrano, sopressata Calabrese and chorizo Soria". For lunch we raided the aging closet. There were dozens of salami and hams hanging from François' busy November workshop as well as some of Nate's recent products. A layer of fine white mold coated most of the meats. We tried several from November for lunch put up against some of Nate's and a few from a Bosnian "salumiere" down in California who's national trademark seems to be the addition of a light smoking to every product.

Once again I immersed myself in the subject at hand. Nate's coffee infused salami was tasty and according to François technically very well finished. The Bosnian meats barely got a nod. François questions why they must smoke everything they make. By the time we were finished I was anticipating an ice-cold pint of Midnight Sun Porter.

Friday April 20, 2012

Work proceeds well. As the team member with baking skills I've been in the corner making dough for our "pâté en croute" and a bit of bread for a sophisticated pig in a blanket, "saucisson de Lyon en brioche". I can't help feel it was also my knife skills that got me the job. Our dry cured products, the salami and hams will not be ready for this weeks banquet but there are plenty of choices hanging in the box from November's team. But our fresh pork products are coming along just fine. The Frankfurter's emulsification was rich and smooth. They poached off with a delightful snap on the first bite. Our selection of "pâté" includes centers of pork liver or pork tenderloin marinated in Courvoisier. The "rillettes" will be smooth and sit nicely with the baguettes we will get from the uncompromisingly good Fire Island Bakery in Anchorage. The stock for the headcheese is a translucent amber color and when cold it is solid enough to bounce a dime on.

We gathered around the large bowl chopper several times today and stuck our hand into it while it was spinning. How else can you get the feel for the conditioning of the lean meat as it chops and turns? After batches of "saucisson de Lyon, chorizo", frankfurter" and "salame nostrano" my hands began to understand the change that meat proteins go through with the addition of salts and the mechanical action of chopping. It gains almost a doughy consistency before the addition of the rest of the ingredients. We had our hands in bowls of fresh pigs blood while we prepared three gallons of "boudin noir". We followed our leader and tasted the blood for flavor. In fact we tasted each and every force meat, before it went to the casings. Tomorrow is our last morning to finish and assemble our menu. It went well today so we don't anticipate too much work on Saturday.

Saturday April 21, 2012

Several steps are required to make a proper "pâté en croute". There is the pie dough and it's handling, there is the "pâté" and it's garnishes and after baking there is the addition of the aspic or jelly to fill the gaps inside created by steam between the crust and filling. If there is a problem in the early part of the process a simple job becomes a complex chain of repairs and half-assed triage. Fortunately I am an expert at half-assed triage. The dough made with freshly rendered lard was stunning in it's flavor, texture and handling qualities. The pâté was fresh and delicately seasoned. The trouble started as it baked. It expanded from the heat in the oven and upon cooling contracted leaving fault-lines and crevasses' across the top and down the sides of the assembly. No time to ruminate on what I did wrong, how would I be able to fill the gaps in my terrines with jelly if it was all going to leak out? How could I serve this? Am I going to let down the team? It was essentially a plumbing problem. I needed to plug the holes in the crust before pouring in the warm aspic. A bit of raw pie dough might patch a small hole but these terrines looked like a train wreck. I unmolded each terrine and lifted it gently onto a sheet of saran wrap careful to put all the dough pieces back in the same place they started.

Mitigate the damage. Work with your back to the chef. It was all coming back to me now from my days at the CIA. Francois walked passed at one point when the "pâté" lay on the table looking like road-kill. Wisely he walked on. Once enveloped completely in Saran I slid them back into the mold and injected them with aspic from a narrow funnel. The finished slices will look perfect on the silver platters as they enter the dining room, if they chill in time.

Saturday evening April 21, 2012

We transferred our finished products to the Turkey Red restaurant. Jason and Stephan blended in with the kitchen and crew and got our tightly rolled "porchetta" roasts into the oven. As they cooked we helped prepare the rest of the food. We laid out platter after platter of sliced "salumi". The "pâté" firmed up and sliced well. After those last couple hours in the kitchen we straightened our hair, took off our aprons and tucked in our shirttails to sit down in the dining room and enjoy our food with some of Turkey Reds best customers. We ate like kings and had a wine paired with every course. After dinner we retired to an Alaskan saloon close by to unwind and toast our teacher and hosts.

We add starter cultures to our "salumi" recipes to create a healthy environment where great new flavors develop. François handled our workshop like he mixes a good salami. He infused his participants with valuable wisdom of his art and craft. And for good measure, he inoculated us with a longing for the small farm and the neighborhood "salumiere". He shared his vision of an economy more palatable than the sterile factory feeding that fills our stomach today.

I'm home now making arrangements to assist a farmer with finishing his pig for slaughter and trying to find out where I can get a hold of a quart or two of fresh pig blood and a supply of rendered lard.

Tom

If we look at the big picture, we can see what is going on in our American meat and sausage world, the mainstream is showing some depressing vistas. Luckily, there are some eddies, some counter currents gaining strength. Enlightened artisans and eclectic palates are building the counter current.

THE STATE OF THE INDUSTRY

We have just about lost the sensible heritage of the tradition to science and technology. The sense of true quality is lost.

The current state of affairs in the American meat industry shows an extreme case of distortion. Technology and science are guiding the extremely concentrated industry to produce for "safety", as defended by the government, as well as convenience for mass distribution, by providing long shelf life using synthetic packaging. This system uses lots of energy and accumulates plastic trash; it attempts to control bacterial infections, but may be compromising general health.

The whole system is necessarily set up and geared to supply economical and "safe" (basically sterilized, "dead") products. It implies convenience in packaging and extremely long shelf life, which is demanded by the distributors and retailers. The consequence is lost freshness and huge amounts of garbage packaging.

Why is it so now? At a time when in all the other parts of the food and beverage industry, we see in reaction to the same trends, a welcomed and much needed renewal of the craftsmanship and the creation of a great variety of products of very high quality. Why is this not happening in the meat industry?

Is it because meat implies the slaughter of animals, while all other food derives from vegetal that can be reaped without spilling blood?

Still, there is no escape to acknowledging that food, to sustain life, demands a sacrifice of life. This is a fundamental mystery, which we are ignoring. We seem to have lost this awareness and sensibility. Are we just dealing with stuff and price?

The simple fact is that it just takes some traveling and the tasting of traditional Old World "jamon", "salame" or "pâté" to discover that something is really missing here. The direct experience of the genuinely delicious, makes, by contrast, our industrial products look, feel, and taste miserable.

Luckily, there are chefs, whose job it is to express their taste buds and refine quality, who are discovering and exploring the missing world of the European tradition. It started in the vineyards and on the family farms, in the dairies, the bakeries, the breweries and the kitchens.

New artisans re-discover the primacy of sensitivity for the art of preparing food. They are re-discovering ancient crafts.

Today, in their kitchens, numerous chefs are making sausages, experimenting with "charcuterie", "salumi" or "Wurst".

In America, there is no place to teach the ancient craft of the sacrifice, butchering and making sausage in the way of the art, the craft and skill of the Artisan.

PURPOSE

The purpose of this work is to help the candidate apprentice to connect with the core values and to master the ancient art of the master sausage maker.

Soul reigns in finesse over knowledge and experience to achieve perfection.

LIFE PROCEEDS FROM LIFE

All our food comes from living organisms in many forms. Salt has been added forever as the only mineral ingredient.

Today, the industry is using numerous chemical additives and/or preservatives, though most of them are still extracted from plants, algae, microbes or other living organisms.

Life is very complex and intricate in its cycles and chains, involving continuous transitions and interferences. No bread, wine, beer, cider, pickle, vinegar, yogurt, sauerkraut, cheese, salami and many other foods or beverages would exist without living ferments transforming the raw ingredients. No refined flavor or textures exists without the play of natural enzymes, produced by a vast microbial environment while aging prosciutto, salami, cheese and many other foods or condiments.

From the gathering instinct to the deliberate choice which goes into the development of crafts in order to prepare and process, our food has evolved by experience, by trial and error, selected and refined by tradition.

We relate to food with all of our senses as we approach, take in and absorb a meal. The look, smell, sound, touch, mouth-feel, aroma, taste, aftertaste, tummy's feeling: all of them help us qualify the food. The finesse of our living instrumentation is immediate and effective. It is with these "tools" that we were able to develop crafts and their products. If we can recognize, educate and refine our senses, we can qualify ourselves to become masters.

The raw sensory input, filtered by sensitivity and finesse, allows for the progressive refinement of the material and the process. Human societies develop in this way and refine with the accumulation of experience, the crafts and the traditions, which form the substance of the culture.

Time tested methods, recipes, craftsmanship, traditions and even rituals, when observed, are able to maintain an efficient and natural balance of hygiene and immunity in society.

Food is thus shaped in function of the resources, territory and climate; it becomes an element of identity together with shelter, clothing, language and beliefs.

As long as the awareness of the living connection is intimate in its mysteries, the sacrifice of life for life is at the core of the sacred. The ritual meal is and stays an essential part of the cultural life. With the development of science, objective measurements progressively replace with abstract information the direct subjective relation and experience. The traditional ways are altered with the progression of analytical knowledge and our relationship to it. A mental process dealing with a perception of reality replaces the direct sensory relation/experience. Quantity of "stuff", replaces Quality. The new paradigm eventually leads to dealing purely with numbers and its ultimate result/conclusion is in the management of production by and for the "bottom line".

Creativity is overcome by greed; quality is lost; and, errant consumers loose their balance, and get sick.

Progressively time tested ways get contested and the connection to the whole of life desintegrates. The food gets identified by the name of it components, proteins, fats, starches, minerals, vitamins. The intimate, sensorial, spiritual connection gets lost and is replaced by mental images, which are manipulated for the sake of advertisement. The mind deals with abstractions disconnected from life itself.

Quality, that, which we can experience, in balance with Life, is replaced by **Quantity** and the satisfaction of emotions more or less rationalized, with some "scientific" input into what we accept as nutrition and hygiene changing values.

Interestingly, we observe the continuous shift of fads and fears affecting the current food and diet culture. We are loosing the collective and individual soul-sensory direct connection with life, replaced by mental abstractions in shifting beliefs.

Is it possible today to stay directly connected to life, while including our "scientific" understanding of the elements, the pieces and parts, the microbes, yeasts and molds, beneficial or pathogenic, the physical exchanges in temperature or hygrometry, the chemical role of salt and additives?

Can we encompass the direct awareness of life, soul sensitivity and mind?

Can we retrieve the balance, the dynamic of true quality?

After all, it is just a matter of our identity, just a matter of respect of our true nature. Spirit, Soul and Mind.

Berkshires at Stone Barns, New York.

HOW CAN WE RE-CONNECT TO QUALITY?

How can we regain respect for the meat from our animals, revive the craft of the sausage maker?

"Saucisson de Lyon".

Let us learn from the "charcutier, salumiere" or "Wurstmeister" of the tradition.

Let us observe the timeless principles; learn what understanding we get from science; let us review all the steps from the farm to the plate.

Macelleria Falorni in Greve, Tuscany.

PRESERVING MEAT

With the occasional kill, there arises an immediate question to the hunter:

How to keep and preserve the meat?

… In the steaming jungles, the primitives roast the prey immediately so that it will keep until they can return to their settlement.

… In a hot Mexico rancho, with no electricity, boiling the meat for hours until it shreds from the bones, does it. Pulled from the bones, the meat is set to evaporate and cool. It will be put in a linen bag to keep the flies away and to let it further dry naturally, to eventually cook into the daily burritos for the next couple of weeks.

… Indians of yore pounded the flesh of the game with berries and exposed thin layers of the mixture to the sun to dry into pemmican to be saved for the lean season.

… In the great North, the salmons are filleted, slashed to expose the flesh and let to dry in the cool air to save rich nutritious food for the long winter.

… On the ancient farm, in colder climes, the winter slaughter takes advantage of the natural refrigeration for a while. What is not consumed for the feast in the following days is put in salt to cure and later smoked or dried and will age in the cellar and the attic.

To dehydrate has forever been and still is the fundamental principle for the preservation of meat.

Removing the water bound to the proteins of the muscle prevents the development of germs, stops the decay and allows for storage.

The fresh dry air, heat applied in various forms, or salt rubbed dry or in brine can absorb the water from the meat.

Over millennia processes have been refined in different forms and resulted in a multitude of products from the simplest to the most complex. A seasonal rhythm, commands the production processes and products are designed for consummation in their own season. Instead "Shelf life " is a modern concept. It relates to the current distribution system of foods in supermarkets and convenience for the consumer. The industry is under constant pressure to increase the duration at great risk for quality and even, unfortunately, for safety.

It was critical to know how to best use every part of the animal. It was done with a very ecological economy of means. Our current mode of cheap, convenient over-abundance wastes a lot of resources.

- Blood has to be consumed immediately or within a few days when prepared and cooked as blood sausage.
- Feet, tail and snouts, cured and cooked make collagen rich meals.
- Skins complete and balance beans dishes and soups and make delicious aspics.
- Organs are best made into a kind of pudding, flavored with fresh herbs and wrapped in cowl fat to be pan fried already on the day of butchering to sustain

the working crew. Organs with some fat and meat can be cured and baked into pâtés good for a few weeks.

- Small meats and trimmings, made into sausage, keep for several weeks, if cured, smoked or somewhat dried.

- Trimmed shoulder muscles and the best hard fat made into salami, cured and fermented, then dried, can age for months.

- Cured, smoked or dried, belly properly kept in larder or cantina, can keep for many months, as bacon, "speck" or "pancetta".

- The nobler muscles of the neck and shoulder, cured as "coppa", or "spalla" will age and keep from winter to summer.

- The whole leg, as "prosciutto", will age and keep a whole year or more.

Preserved dry cured meat

SALUMI, CURED, FERMENTED AND SMOKED MEATS AND OTHER FERMENTED FOODS.

Salami and prosciutto introduces us to the Italian word "SALUMI", more than only salami, (plural of salame in Italian). The word "salumi" covers all the products that can be crafted by the "salumierc". They are all the typical meat products of the Mediterranean culture. Italian, Hispanic, French, Slav of the Balkans and cven Middle Eastern cultures, antedating the arrival of the Muslims, have refined the preserving of mostly pork meats into art. Jews and Muslims do it with cow, donkey, camel, sheep and goat.

From the Middle East to Spain the art of curing, fermenting, aging or smoking meats evolved in a multitude of very ancient products. The roots of meat preserving have been lost in time with our hunter ancestors. The advent of animal domestication some ten millennia ago, with sheep, pig, goat, cattle, horse, camel, and llama gave regular access to meat. Milking also was added to hunting and butchering. The art of preserving meat was extended to cheese making. With the beginning of agriculture, wine, bread, cheese, "salumi" and all the other fermented food appeared.

Over millennia, animals, meats, ingredients, methods and recipes evolved as the result of intuition, observation and experience. Craftsmen relied on the refined instruments of our five senses, long before the advent of the laboratory and the development of science.

The fermented essences of a perfect meal.

We recognize today with our scientific knowledge that the craftsmen of old had found the right way to influence the natural balance of physics, chemistry and biological life to produce their masterworks.

All encompassing harmony

The "salumiere" learned and cultivated the art of how to create appealing and delicious products available in all seasons. They learned to take advantage of ingredients, salts and spices. They also mastered the skill of using natural containers like guts and bladders. They practiced sustainable ecology before the invention of the concept.

They learned to use particular conditions of temperature and relative humidity to control the naturally occurring fermenting germs, yeasts and molds to assist in the miracle of refining taste, flavors and texture. For that purpose, they knew how to use the moist and warm kitchen to launch the natural fermenting and curing process. They found the ideal moment at which to open the window for the fresh breeze to dry the sausage or the cured meats and to find the right conditions in the attic or the cellar to age and mature the "salumi".

Elsewhere in the Germanic forests, the "Wurstmeister" would know how to generate the perfect smoke to flavor and to preserve his sausages, learning to respect the same principles of humidity, temperature and time.

A great finesse of attention is necessary to achieve perfection. It demands the workings of the soul with lots of care, using refined senses, skilled handling and a sharp mind to achieve the expression of true quality.

The apprentice had to go patiently through all the activities of the shop to gain his skills under the guidance of a master and to gain his qualification as a worker. To progress, he had to travel making a "Grand Tour" to gain experience with more masters in very different places and circumstances and eventually, to mature to become recognized as one of them after the performance of his masterwork or "chef d'oeuvre".

The quest of the apprentice was framed and supported by the existence of the guild or association of the masters of the trade who determined the qualification of the "compagnon" and, eventually, that of a master.

Monsieur Reynon, Traiteur.

Jean Plasse, Charcutier.

Signor Capoferri, Salumiere.

Industrial meat products

Today, we are losing the capacity to experience quality. Our living instrumentation is still available but neglected. Authority has been delegated to the instruments of the lab and to the technicians. We have replaced our immediate, direct sensory experiencing with a reflective mental function. The creator becomes subservient to the system driven by the computer.

With the predominance of scientific rationale and over-regulation in the industry of today, we have moved away from expertise and from the personal and direct sensory evaluation of our food. We have fallen into an illusory world of mental information and images of what we believe and, hence perceive to be real; what is supposed to taste good. This is the result of our current system of values with the perception of life and reality abstracted in scientific symbolism and measured by monetary value.

During the last 50 years, the meat industry, abandoning centuries of ancient craftsmanship, has changed direction. It has moved into the direction opposite from the old wisdom. The change has been imposed by the cultural shift from quality to quantity, i.e., by the economy of the "bottom line" or to rephrase "It's the stupid economy".

More for less

The dominance of price as the most important value justifies the need for increased productivity, concentration in higher volume and the development of technologies and methods guided by science and supported by marketing techniques63. This has allowed for abundance or rather overabundance today but has left out of the equation the overabundant creation of trash from packaging and wrapping, pollution, poor nutrition, poor health and depravity of taste.

The old ways

The ancient economy commands to value and to consume the whole animal. We still tell the joke about the old truth:

In pork the only un-edible is the "oink"
That was the ideal, ecological approach. Today it is lost. Blood, innards and even the precious fat are excluded from our table; instead, they are re-processed and fed to other

animals, which sometimes creates nasty closed circuits with sometimes nightmarish consequences, when unwilling animals are fed remains of their own kind (remember the mad cow disease).

Scientific knowledge and economic pressure have driven the modern meat industry into a paradox:

Animals, which were bred in harmony with nature and selected for their rusticity and quality, have by now been genetically modified to increase their productivity. The apparent economic gain, measured in dollars per pound, ignores completely the aspect of true quality and has led to ecological disasters. The pork industry, having lost all of what made pork succulent, had to launch a new marketing category and concept of "The Other White Meat" to influence consumers.

The principle of dehydrating to preserve is now replaced by the injection of liquids supplemented by phosphates, to bind the water into the proteins. The chemical process is complemented by a physical tumbling, by a massage of sorts, which is added to the process in order to transform the muscle into a kind of tender, hydrated Jello.

These high-water modern meat products, be they turkey breast, roast-beef or ham, have a lower cost since water is cheap. But they are highly perishable and thus, potentially at risk of contamination; not only are they fragile but they also tend to be tasteless.

The production technology demands the addition of all kind of preservatives, extenders, flavoring and coloring in order to retain some acceptability. To reach satisfaction when eating, the diluted meats have to be consumed in larger quantity. Nowadays, it takes at least one inch of any meat between the bread slices and lots of condiments to make an acceptable sandwich.

Fancy flavorings are used to compensate for the fundamental unsatisfactory quality. More or less added water defines the price value. The original meat is hardly recognizable anymore. Fancy labels instead create an identity.

A few college-educated specialists with theoretical formation, command mostly uneducated equipment operators. Complex computer driven systems demand the attention of technicians, versed in electronics, with too little attention given to the substance.

Meat and products are known abstractly as measurable components: water/protein/fat ratios, PH, salt content, aW value, critical temperature, etc.

The marketing pressure is on cost and cosmetic appearance; too little, for lack of skill or attention, is paid to quality.

This evolution of the technology and intense marketing pressure lead to the concentration of production in an ever-growing volume. The complexity of movement of animals and meats throughout a huge market has caused the development, on scientific grounds, of the new discipline of sanitizing. The guiding principle is to eliminate all germs, good and bad, launching in consequence all kinds of mostly toxic chemicals in the environment.

The new hygiene allowing for the quasi-sterile processing of foods, with the now common use of stabilizing agents, leads to the possibility of largely extending the shelf life of packaged food. This trend responds to a constant pressure of the distributors. The new product, enclosed in packaging practically sterile with a high water content, implies the risk of massive contamination if, by accident, pathogens are introduced during processing.

This new situation inadvertently eliminates the opportunity of sustaining our immune system with the more natural residual germ content of traditional methods.

A whole new industry of packaging has been created to protect fragile products to allow for the shelf life requirement of mass production and distribution. It may allow for bacterially protected products, but, because of the long time involved, it tends to yield stale products to the consumer and creates a tremendous amount of packaging waste.

The modern deli meat counter.

"Norcineria" on "Campo dei Fiori", Rome.

The tradition instead better respects life balance:

- On the farm, the animals are respected, living in a natural and sustainable environment. They are selected and bred for their quality.

- Craftsmen take responsibility for the meat, the ingredients, the casings, the machines and the processes. They have been trained in the traditional way, with a full knowledge of the animal's anatomy, skilled in the ability to bone and trim each muscle to its proper usage knowing how to condition and prepare all the meat and organs for the specific product. ***They are able to use the whole of the animal.***

- They are able to work with sharp knives, simpler instruments and machines; they are master of their technique; they have a full understanding of the role of ingredients, the cure, the fermentation, the drying, the smoking or cooking.

- All their attention is on the perfection of quality, goodness and elegance, on the look, texture, flavor and aroma of a perfect product.

- Quality of the meat is essential for the quality of the product. It requires better and more mature meats from healthy adult animals, bred under natural and sustainable conditions on the farm.

- Hygiene in the product is achieved with methods to handle meats and cleaning with the ability, sense and skill to maintain a balanced bacterial environment augmenting the role of the beneficial germs, competing with and reducing the detrimental ones. The beneficial bacteria are allowed time in natural processes like fermentation, curing and dehydrating to yield wholesome and naturally flavored products.

- More time, specific to each phase of production, is given for the curing, the fermenting and enzymatic aging to develop the proper texture, taste and flavor at maturity. The added time in aging also enhances the digestibility and the nutritional value of the meats.

- The stability of the product is achieved naturally and ecologically by the method and the time involved, without any ingredients and chemicals other than salt, saltpeter (nitrate), sugar and natural spices and the managed help of the incurring micro-organisms.

- Freshness is an essential value and guarantee of the goodness of products. Shorter distribution lines and knowledgeable service staff in the store can support the product with advice to educate the consumer, and manage the products according to their natural shelf life.

- The price of better quality meat and production cost are higher, but the packaging cost can be saved. The traditional product value is much higher with no added water, healthier meats, higher concentrated nutrition and rich natural aroma and flavor.

- "Less but better" ends up being largely beneficial to the consumer.

CHARCUTIER, SALUMIERE, WURSTMEISTER
THE NEW MASTER SAUSAGE MAKER

In the European Tradition, these names designate in three different languages, in three different cultures, the same mastery: the art of sausage making.

Same values, expressed in different way.

In Italy, il "salumiere", also called "norciniere", is the master of the art of making "salumi", mostly from the meat of mature animals. The tradition is characterized by very mellow fermentation and long aging, incorporating centuries of refinement to achieve pleasure and satisfaction at the table. The "prosciutto", "mortadella", "cotechino" and "salame" have conquered the world.

The Spaniards share the same tradition and skill, colored by the pervasive use of the "pimenton", that incredibly aromatic paprika - "dulce" or "picante".

I hold in high esteem the "pimenton de la Vera", a very special paprika dried and delicately smoked on wood fire.

Spanish nobles governed the kingdom of Naples in what is now southern Italy and Sicily, where the "pepperoncini" also reign in the local "salumi" like the "sopressata". Likewise, the classic "salame Napolitano" is flavored with aromatic peppers and lightly smoked.

The "salchichoner" of Catalonia make the famous "salchichon de Vich" and every province has their "jamon" and "chorizo". They know how to develop a richer aroma in their product, adjusting to a warmer clime and working, maturing and aging with their hot sun.

"Jamon Iberico de belota," made with the "pata negra" black pigs, which fatten from acorns in Estremadura, or the ubiquitous "jamon serrano', allow Spaniards to be the largest consumers of dry cured ham as a staple of "tapas".

The French "charcutier" (literally the cooker of meats), is much closer to the art of the "chef de cuisine". "Pâtés", "galantines", "andouilles", "boudins" and "jambons" achieve a marvelous combination of visual and gastronomical delicacy, culminating in the presentation of the "chef d'oeuvre" (the master work, which culminates the achievement of an apprentice, who graduates as a "compagnon"), to get the recognition of the mastery.

Charcutier. Salumiere. Wurstmeister.

The Germanic "Wurstmeister" expresses his superb knowledge of the alchemy of transmuting meats and fats into the golden perfection of a superbly smoked sausage. Many combinations of meats, spices, textures, flavors and shapes are the pride of every region. The south of Germany, Austria and Switzerland are home to mostly emulsified sausages – "Frankfurter", "Wiener", "Bockwurst", "Bratwurst", "Cervelat" and many others. In the north and east, the tradition is for coarser, smoked sausages like the "Braunschweiger", "Debrecziner", "Krakauer" (all named after a city) and all the fermented, smoked "Dauerwurst" of Westphalen.

Smoking can be short and hot combined with cooking for many different "Wurst". It can be done slowly, cold smoking at a lower temperature and often repeated over a longer period for uncooked products like the dried "Katenschinken" and "Speck", which are smoked cousins to the Mediterranean "prosciutto". In Italy, in the same tradition, the German-speaking province of Bolzano produces the famous "speck Tirolese".

In Eastern and Northern Europe, the Slav, Russian, Polish and Balkan tribes maintain very rich traditions of sausages and meats with many more local specialties.

The European Union has sanctioned the originality and the value of distinct traditional and regional products. To be recognized, the specification of the product has to be established by a consortium of the local manufacturers, thus, creating the authority, which defines and protects the originality of the DOP label.

This system, which is anchored in tradition, warrants the respect of quality demanded by the European consumer.

Daunting task to follow the French and Italian using lower case for common names and Germans using the uppercase! And then, "quote"s for all these foreign names, not knowing which ones have already been assimilated by our US lingo.

The community owns and protects its products; quality and regional tradition are the essence.

Founders of the American Meat Industry

Smoking and cooking are the characteristics of the type of sausages that German and Polish immigrant "Wurstmeister" brought to America. As original founders of the U.S. Meat Industry, they set the standard for our hot dog, bacon and other franks.

A few "salumieri" immigrants, as well, are at the origin of our dry salami, genoa, sopressata and prosciutto made in America.

From the American farming tradition, we still have the country hams of Virginia. From the Cajuns we can also enjoy the "andouille" and "chaurice".

Unfortunately, U.S. business seems to be more concerned by brand value than quality.

In Europe, the strength of the culture and tradition still demand from the industry to respect the quality of the ancient craft even if the trade has evolved driven by science and technology.

In America, instead, whatever artful craft had managed to emigrate with the founders of the industry has mostly been lost. It was progressively superseded by other values, which are fundamental to the American culture.

Quality is lost to quantity.

Today, unfortunately, the price is perceived as the only value. The American food industry leads the world in terms of efficiency and supplies the consumers with very cheap but quality-poor food.

The bulk of the economy is driven by pressure on price, which demands constant increase in productivity. The meat industry follows the pattern, using all the resources of abundant energy, technology, scientific knowledge, economies of scale, with enormous concentration in animal factories, slaughterhouse, packing plants, distribution and retail.

In this way and over time, the sensory connection with the reality of life on the farm and along with it the creative, responsible and integral role of the craftsman, has been replaced by technology, offering speed, mass production and the mediocre lower common denominator as the standard.

We have lost our own direct sense of what is good and healthy and must have fallen passively into the manipulations of biased information supplied by the media, by advertising, which promoted scares and fads.

As we are educated and culturally driven by the want for more and an illusion of saving, we ignore or neglect our own senses, our capacity to experience what defines quality in its living sense. We follow and accept as our own beliefs and reality, the mental ideas and images pumped on us.

The big, U.S. meat industry has replaced craftsmanship with technology. Poultry, pork and beef, and soon fish are factory produced, mass killed and broken into commodity-meats at the lowest possible cost. Their meat is moved around the whole continent, often blended and loosing any connection with their origin.

Americans have lost the old necessity to valorize and consume the whole of the animal; only some muscles and little fat ends up on our table. What we can't export to less sophisticated markets is re-cycled by the feed industry into feeds for more animal meat for our consumption.

The intimate contact of the artisan with the matter as a living whole, kept in balance with the environment has been replaced by a scientific abstraction of the World. The perception of the meat is reduced into water, proteins and lipids; the living environment, into germs, bacteria, molds and yeast. Sanitation, now a paradigm for the industry, is attempting to destroy the whole bacterial life, good and bad, associated with the process.

The experience of the substance, the re-cognition of its quality, has been mutated into the image of the brand; in the store, the product itself is hardly visible to the consumer; it disappears, masked behind the label, covered in a tight package. The information, required by the labeling regulations, feeds the mind with abstract information about the content of the product.

The meat is no longer seen, smelled or tasted; it is known only by information.

Without connection to the product, the senses are out; the mental information is in.

Our minds themselves are confused by a constant flow of information, dramatizing, changing and conflicting themes relating to particular aspects. Scares are orchestrated and sensationalized in accordance with marketing opportunities into the fad of the moment - vitamins, cholesterol, saturated-fats, omega-3 are recent themes. Words like "natural", "clean", "" are often abused.

All those fading trends or temporary beliefs are promoted as quality factors by the media to the point of distracting the consumers from relating to the product itself via the direct experience of the senses: seeing, smelling, touching, chewing, tasting, feeling a satisfied stomach, feeling vitalized by the right meal.

On the way to material abundance, we have shifted from balanced and discriminating usage, to dreaming of abstract, relatively cheap "stuff" that we over consume without really connecting.

The time is now ripe for an awakening. The pendulum has swung far and is coming back.

Chefs training in Palmer, 2012.

Well... we are now masters of productivity; we trust Science; we compete for the "buck" but we are not too happy with what we find to eat in the deli department.

Charcutier. Salumiere. Wurstmeister.

A RENAISSANCE IS HAPPENING

Passionate individuals are discovering anew and exploring the real living world of the "salumi", "charcuterie" and "Wurst".

The fermented foods, - wine, cheese, bread, pastry, brew, pickle and preserve - have preceded meats in the great renewal.

As a young butcher-farmer trainee on my first trip to America in 1958, I was thrilled to discover hamburger, floats, malts and pancakes. I was overwhelmed at the size of T-bone steaks of still incomparable beef, but wine was worst than the worst, bread was loaded with stuff and vitamins was sticking to my teeth. There was no cheese other than mushy cheddar or bland Swiss. The only decent restaurants were steakhouses with their humongous Idaho potatoes, edible only when soaked in butter.

What a change since those days for the major part of the menu; but still, meat and its products are lagging behind. Actually, in many ways the situation is much worse than 50 years ago.

Now is the time for the meat products to regain the fundamentals of true quality.

However bad the current situation is, it has to come back to quality. The animal production is distorted by the Washington politics of subsidies to the production of corn and soy, which depreciate the grass as the natural feed for meat.

The industry itself is tied in knots by the powers of the food regulation and control authority. Packers are dominated by the retailing giants, which impose a constant pressure to compete over price, ignoring substance. The focus is on the race for increased productivity or convenience, ever more sophisticated machinery or chemistry meant to lower cost or to increase shelf life much to the detriment of quality.

Inertia, consequence of the size of very large entities and patterns, prevents much renewal in the system.

Times are changing. We are, as a cultured society, awakening to a new, wider look at our environment. We consider new values of sustainability, humane husbandry and handling of animals, and natural or organic growing methods are the new focus.

The abuse of technology is bringing a growing awareness and a nascent respect for the unity of life and ecology. This revolution, started some time ago in the United States,

66

is gaining ground. The other food categories led the way, starting most visibly 40 or 50 years ago with wines in California, cheese in New England and Wisconsin, expanding to the whole world of gourmet food, together with the changing dining scene.

The big meat industry has shown only limited change. Instead, the movement to renew meat products started elsewhere: chefs in their kitchens felt the call for better meats and started to experiment on their own. Chefs by definition cultivate their sensory finesse and are stimulated to innovate, to create. In their less regulated environment they are free to explore, to discover and to renew the craft of ancient artisans.

Chefs travel extensively exploring the world of food. They have tasted in Europe incomparable meats. They have smuggled some samples back home and tried to re-produce the recipes and the ways of old.

Successful in their kitchens, the more enterprising have started to produce their own "salumi" or "charcuterie"; some have even launched new factories. Their concern for quality has led them to connect with farmers who had preserved ancient breeds of animals from the time when quality was the only purpose and sustainability the only way.

The new explorers, chefs and artisans are launching innovative new products of their own and most of the time, they actually re-create ancient recipes. They find new meat, new association of ingredients and new combinations appear in creative dishes.

This renewal is made possible by the rebirth of the sustainable family farm, where ancient types of animals are bred. These breeds have been selected for their eating quality and rusticity. They grow in a natural environment without pollution or the systematic use of drugs. They produce in growing abundance the meat, which had just about disappeared, chased from our tables by the "other white meat".

This new movement is part of a larger resurgence of local produce and heirloom vegetables and fruits, which can be found nowadays in a multitude of farmers' markets. It is sustained by the growing demand for local, natural, fresh food.

The genuine is re-born for the taste buds of real food lovers eager to discover the new products on the menu of restaurants and specialty stores.

These new, dedicated artisans and farmers demonstrate an awakening of their souls - the source of finesse - directing their senses, feelings and emotions and simultaneously balancing the rationalizing, knowing mind, which is thus able to put to good use all of the knowledge of science within a new sensitivity for quality and harmony with our environment.

CRAFT, TECHNIQUE, SCIENCE AND EXPERIENCE

This work will attempt to share the essence of the art, the philosophy and the principles of true quality. It is addressed to those moved in their souls by the desire to do good and who are willing to revive the traditions of the "charcutier", "salumiere" and "Wurstmeister" as craftsmen of different cultures.

It will be essential here to shift from the paradigm of numbers, of quantity as symbol and purpose to the direct-sensory experience of quality.

From quantity to quality

Many recipes can be found elsewhere. Herewith, you will find 40 basic ways of valorizing the whole pig. You will also find references to sources of recipes in the index. We expect the student or, dare we hope and better yet, the **apprentice** to develop with confidence the capacity and the skill to create her or his own recipes and techniques.

We need instead to learn finesse and discover the principles at work. Let's fully understand what is going on in the processes to become the master of the art.

The field is extremely vast to explore: beginning at the farm with the animals, leading to sacrificing, butchering, fabricating, processing in all its complexity, to maturing all the way to cooking, serving and eating.

Anatomy, physiology, biology, and microbiology can inform and explain all the aspects of processing: preparing the meats, cutting, grinding, emulsifying, resting, stuffing, salting, curing, smoking, fermenting and aging.

Physics and thermodynamics rule the matter and the environment; they explain cooking, cooling, drying and the necessary conditions of the environment for maturing.

Chemistry explains the interaction and reaction of ingredients.

All the science, though, is not sufficient by itself to master the craft. As proof, we can observe that scientists don't generally excel in crafting sausages. It would actually be beyond their specialized understanding.

We require instead the capacity to use in a sensible way scientific information and, fundamentally, to be in direct connection with the substance and its life. More importantly, we have to develop the practice, experience and sensibility resulting in skill and, ultimately, developing the finesse and follow the intuition to deal with the meats, the ingredients and the process.

Achieving intelligence

Apprentices need time to share with masters, starting their initiation with the menial tasks to accumulate experience and to build knowledge. They need great patience to train and to develop skill. They will need to travel and learn in different contexts, with time to accumulate knowledge and practice to mature to mastery, until, as it is for the performing artist, the score is no longer needed and the playing comes from the heart.

The list is quite long of the different matters, crafts, processes, materials, ingredients, tools, instruments and machines with which the apprentice will need to get familiar in order to perform.

We will examine them separately, conveying as much as possible the fundamental principles and categories. Our purpose is to develop the familiarity with all aspects and their implications in all sequences of any process. The aim is to achieve a freedom of creation, allowing the apprentice to progressively develop his or her own techniques and capacities instead of a rote teaching of how to do things.

LEARNING CHAPTERS

Meat, Butchering and Fabricating.

Cuts and Trims.

Spices. Ingredients. Salting.

Chopping. Grinding. Mixing.

Activation of the Proteins and Emulsifying. Stuffing.

Injecting and tumbling (*Devil's Work*).

Casings. Twine and Nets. Binding.

Fermenting. Smoking. Cooking. Molding. Aging.

Packaging.

Charcutier. Salumiere. Wurstmeister.

Computing Control.

Slicing. Tasting.

Cleaning.

Master and apprentices, Palmer, 2012.

ANIMALS

The animals, which provide us with their bodies, are sensitives creatures; their life is influenced by the environment, by the care and harmony provided to them. They too are what they eat, the feed provided is extremely important, so is the time they are allowed to grow and develop. It is important to be able to distinguish the natural way from the industrial process; the defining line is to a large part conditioned by the care that the animal gets or the absence of it.

At 1, as a young butcher, I was into my 3 years of apprenticeship. I also had a passion for farming. I was attending a course at the "Bergerie Nationale de Rambouillet". Learning to tend to flocks of sheep was my way to go beyond the meat, to learn how it came about. The grounds of the "Bergerie Nationale" are part of "le Chateau de Rambouillet", the country residence, near Paris, of the Président de la République.
I remember well Monsieur Moret, the "Chef Berger" telling us that the secret of raising good animals was to provide them "le repos au sein de l'abondance": rest amidst plenty. He put in a few words, the secret of good meat.

There are many different types of domesticated animals; they all derive from a few wild roots, beginning about ten - seven thousand years ago. They are the result of specific breeding over these thousands of years. Today, very different from their wild ancestor, most breeds have adjusted to specific situations. They have adjusted to a particular environment, itself changed from wild to farmed nature. They have been refined into specialized purpose.

A couple of centuries ago, in an age of eclectic values, - the classic age, in Europe, mostly England and France, breeds were selected and refined for their meat quality, conformation and appearance, for their look. In those days, beauty and harmony were the essence of civilization. Cost was a consequence, not yet a purpose, animals were let to mature naturally, following the seasons cycles.

That was before the arrival of our modern times of economic management and scientific technology. The new economic necessities moved the concern of breeding into the hands of zoo-technicians, with a new concern for the development of prolific, more precocious, high-feed converting animals, all things geared for higher yield, concerned by the return on capital more than the satisfaction of good eats. The result, nowadays, are younger, leaner animals, with watery meat. The whole evolution, or shall I say involution, proved very detrimental to quality.

Time is money in modern industrial animal production; fast grown meat is watery and tender, which seems, interestingly, to be the value, besides price, most praised by modern marketing. Of old it was more the taste, texture, succulence of denser, ripe meats that would be allowed to age or mature before consumption.

Large White Hogs.

Here we will limit ourselves to the pork as object of our art.

Edible from the snout to the tail, no other meat comes close to yielding such a variety of succulent products.

MEAT

Economic concentration of the industry in huge quasi-monopolies allowed by scientific and technological "progress" in breeding, feeding and disease control has led to the factory production of the "other white meat" known as the modern pork. This pale meat, of immature animals, is watery, lacks in fat for juiciness and flavor; it

is bland and cannot achieve deliciousness in any way. Geneticists have even been able to add to pigs body two or three ribs to get more valued chops to these "improved breeds". This "efficient" modern type pork, produced massively in confinement with the help of drugs and antibiotics, is indirectly source of nasty pollutions. All in all it is not a very attractive picture.

Instead, classic breeds from past centuries are still around. They had been selected for their quality and capacity to produce fat, when at a time, a couple of centuries ago the occidental pork, descendant of the wild boar, where crossed with the newly discovered, oriental pigs. These hogs were a basic resource of the colonists in America, before the advent of soy and peanut. In a land without olive trees; the lard and bacon were the fats of choice and indispensible commodities.

These old pigs survived and can still be found increasingly in family farms nearly everywhere. They have survived for their quality and adaptation to the traditional farming way. They are kept under more natural and humane conditions, in the renewed ancient sustainable way.

They are the colored types, Berkshire, Hampshire, Duroc, "Cinta Cenese", woolly "Mangalitza" and many other breeds from every province and crossbred like the Farmer's cross, dear to Paul Willis from Thornton in Iowa, who is playing a major role to revive the Midwest tradition with Niman Ranch.

The pigs are let to mature, accumulate more fat. During a longer life and with more exercise in the field, the meat of these pigs becomes marbled, gains succulence, substantially better than the "Other White Meat".

Still their feed conditions the very quality of their fat. It is an essential aspect of the quality of the pork meat. The best breeds, if poorly fed, will gain a soft and oily fat containing mostly unsaturated fatty acids. It is very detrimental to the derived meat products. It is very important to the eating quality and to the processing ability of the meat, to feed the pork in a way to obtain a fat that will crystallize and harden when refrigerated.

In the right pork, you will recognize a fuller, rounder conformation and the brighter, blooming color of the muscle, the bright white firmness and crystallization of the fat, never the paler, yellowish, oily softness of a poorly produced hog. After refrigeration, examine the conformation, the proportion of the carcass, recognize the lean to fat proportion. A good place to look is between the ribs inside the carcass; the ribs should be covered by a light, fatty membrane, while the muscles between the ribs should be visible, signal of a mature and well proportioned meat. If all is white-looking it signals very fat pork, which will require a lot of trimming and poor yield, but certainly of succulent eating quality.

At the other extreme, the excessively lean pork, often immature, will have a better yield but poor eating qualities, typically the case of the "Other White Meat".

An expert eye will distinguish at first glance, the excellent hard from the yellowish, often shiny, soft fat. Finger pressure applied to the back fat will assess its hardness;

A practical way to grade the quality of the fat, is to evaluate the leaf lard one day after slaughter, held in a cooler, still on the carcass or separated. Top quality will be bright white, stiff, hard to crush with the finger. The worst will be yellowish, shiny, oily to the touch and very soft.

The characteristic of the meat and the fat determine to a very dominant part, the quality of the final product. Not only, will the best hard fat yield the best sausages and cured meats, but also will be the most juicy and succulent chop.

Suckling, Runner, Guilt, Barrow, Sow, Boar, Wild Boar, Feral Pig

The members of the porcine family are consumed in all forms and shape, following the local tradition and availability.

Each has a proper use, but for our purpose of fabricating and processing, maturity has the advantage. The guilts seems to cut better than barrows at the common butcher pig size, about 200 Lb. (carcass weight).

The best Italian "salumi" are made from mature (mostly Large White) hogs at 400 Lb.

The French "salaisonier" work mostly with young sows, butchered after 2-3 farrowing and fed another 2-3 months.

If they cannot be castrated in time, boars, because of the strong smell of their meat, are more difficult to use. In this country most end up in "all pork" sausages, mixed with sows.

ANATOMY

The apprentice has to learn how the animal is composed internally and specifically, how each part of the carcass, each muscle, bone and fat tissue is articulated. It is essential to know the specific quality of each muscle and the best usage for it.

Learn the necessary skill to enhance and perfect the inherent qualities of each piece of meat by accurately cutting, boning, trimming and handling properly each cut, at each step of the manufacturing process, from breaking the carcass in respecting its natural divisions, in boning, without slashing and destroying the integrity of the muscles, trimming, sorting, holding and conditioning each part for its proper usage.

Each part of the carcass offers specific usages, from modest sausage to glorious prosciutto, but do not neglect the too often discarded but very valuable offal, including the blood, liver, heart, kidneys, spleen, lungs, tripe, guts, caul fat and the snout, tongue, brain and cheeks from the head.

http://porcine.unl.edu/porcine2005/pages/index. jsp?what=crossectionListMeat composition

A very good understanding of the components of what we designate as meat, in this case, muscle meat, is essential for the mastery of the craft.

Individual muscles or group of muscles forming the "Meat" contain three essential parts, which have very different properties:

- **Muscle fibers** are formed of myosin and actinin, the protein motors of movement. They are grouped in bundles, varying in size depending on the location and function of the muscle; they are connected to the bones on which they leverage by membranes and sinews.

- **Collagen and elastin** tissues, wraps the muscle fiber bundles, attach and contain them with membranes, attaching themselves to bones by tendons, or sinews, wrongly called nerves by butchers. Skin is mostly collagen.

- **Fat** functions as storage of energy. It also cushions the muscles and organs, accumulating in the collagen membranes between the bundles of muscle proteins, under the skin and in the abdomen.

Shoulder has many, rather small, very active muscles with finer fibers. They have more color and tend to be firmer, because, they are supported by dense network of membrane and sinew. On the opposite, muscles from the leg are more massive, with larger muscle fibers and are paler and softer.

The nature of the muscle will command specific usage or demand further fabricating and trimming to fit the requirements of products. Shoulder muscles demand a lot of "de-sinewing" but are best for salami: soft leg muscles fit ham production.

Since the proportions of components of the meat vary with the breed, with age, with life conditions and alimentation, each lot or even individual animal may present different characteristics. For each there will be another way to use it, for each part a corresponding optimum.

There lies a very important professional ensemble of skills: to evaluate the quality of the meat, the ability to break, bone, cut and trim each part: to know how to handle and to process for the best result.

The utmost loving care, attention and respect, at each step of production, are needed to achieve a masterwork.

By now, you must have realized that I am coming from a different place, literally and symbolically.

The World we live in is made of patterns and habits, generally accepted beliefs, written and unwritten rules. All form the World, the environment in which we operate.

Our current state of civilization, more so in this country than anywhere else, is expressing itself, conditioning everything through an optic of science, actually turning everything, every value into numbers, abstract quantities.

This system obviously delivers abundance; abundance of "stuff", but quality goes to pot!

Beyond all the thinking, which produces such modern system, there is life, the soul animating the whole, whatever sense we have of its power through our feelings, intuitions, awareness of beauty and love.

It is enough to face, that plenitude comes from expressing soul through our instrument, in a creative movement.

I am asking you to approach this apprenticeship with an open mind, connecting with the life involved at each step. Develop your awareness of what is. Do not get caught in the abstract knowledge in the theory as realit;, use science to understand life.

Get into the "animus" of the substance.

Be a creator of quality.

The step required is implying responsibility. Be prepared to deal with the interface of the real life and the rules and regulations constructed within the system with the best of intentions, but sometime producing negative effects.

Thank you for coming along this far; now let us examine the "how to".

BUTCHERING

The rustic way.

Today slaughterhouses do the necessary job of converting the pigs into pork. The USDA requirements and inspection of the process have practically eliminated the custom slaughter practice; it should warrant the best handling and hygiene. Properly dressing a pig and garnering all the parts demand a highly skilled attention, which is very difficult to find nowadays.

Remember that only the oink should be wasted! Not so many parts, blood and organs.

The considerate and careful handling during transport to the final destination and the way the kill is done have a determining impact on the appearance and quality of the carcass. The best pig can be ruined into bad pork by brutal handling or suffering during transport.

To the trained eye of the professional, the appearance of the carcass will tell where the best job is done; look for bruises and blood spots, caused by stressful careless handling and stay away from such slaughterhouses.

Quality, destroyed at that stage, can't be recovered. Often unskilled sticking at bleeding time, leaves a lot of clotted blood material on the carcasses, even into the shoulders.

Proper hygiene and refrigeration are also determining factors that demand attention.

Two kinds of operations are available: most common is slaughter skin on, hair together with the epidermis being eliminated by hot water bath or shower or more rarely by hot wax; the alternative is skinning the pig, in order to commercialize the hide. Obviously, this way limits the potential usage - no headcheese, trotter, "cotechino" or prosciutto can be processed for lack of the skin.

Another very important consideration is the gathering of the offal (blood, pluck, intestines, internal organs). Most operations neglect to save the blood or the intestines and save, at best, only the heart and liver from the red organs.

Some split the head and save the tongue and brain; most cut the head straight out, severing the cheek, this reduces the possibility of making full "guanciale".

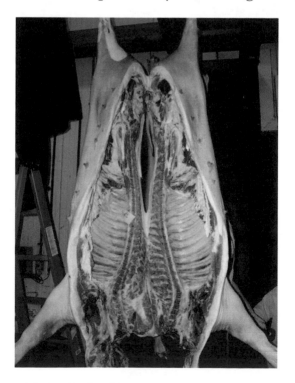

Headless carcass with jowls, leaf lard removed, note the peeling on the left leg.

Shoulder.

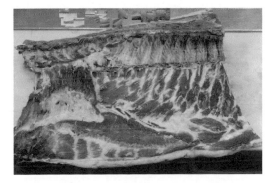

Center, Belly and Loin, w/o Spareribs.

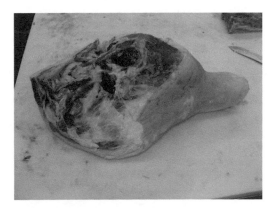

Leg, whole with sirloin and knuckle intact.

Butchering and processing are regulated. USDA sets the rules and controls. It used to be a support activity with inspectors, usually retired butchers controlling the materials and the processes. Nowadays, the responsibility has shifted to the operator, which has to prove, via documentation, following the HCCP procedure, that the product has been submitted to the critical validating steps.

The products themselves have to be tested regularly for bacteriological safety.

These rules and procedures fit the industry, but are overly burdensome for the single operator or the small artisanal operation.

The alternatives are levels of inspection articulated at the State level in many different forms, run by health department for restaurant kitchen or other entities for retail operations run by State, City or County. The result is a jumble of systems and rules, resulting in very different practical situations, with lots of loopholes.

I see the need for a more coherent, more effective system that would take in consideration all the experience of the tradition, to be assisting and controlling the artisanal production.

FABRICATING

This is the stage where the carcass is broken into the primal cuts and eventually trimmed into the meat pieces specified for further processing.

Precise and skilled knife work can maximize the value and improve the total yield of the carcass, if the work is done in anticipation of the final usage.

Unfortunately for us, most industrial packing plants are organized for speed; unskilled labor is used in simplified speedy procedures for the sake of cost control; carcasses are broken in five primal cuts by saws on a conveyor; boning, where required, is done with slashing cuts, ignorant of the precise anatomy.

This method is too coarse, always bent to increase the weight of those parts that are in demand. It mostly ignores the actual structure of muscles and bones; it forces a lot of subsequent fabricating, which generates lots of lesser value trimmings.

The boning of primal cuts like shoulder picnic or ham, poorly done, slashes muscle, which limits their further usage and value.

Instead we can fabricate the carcass more intelligently, using our knowledge of the anatomy, and our professional handling of the knife and saw. Thus, we can achieve a much better yield and use every part for the best possible usage.

With the skill of a surgeon we can fabricate a carcass into the cuts ready for further processing. We can sort and trim muscle and fat in categories fitting for specific products. This is an indispensable skill, which demands serious training and attention.

We control the yield of fabricating in a spreadsheet that you will find under COMPUTING AND CONTROL.

Ref: The depiction of the whole process in the photos of "Breaking the Hog" by Elizabeth Silva. < http://www.francoisvecchio.com >

STANDARD CUTS AND TRIMS

The North American Meat Processors Association, NAMP, has developed standards which specify the major cuts and categories of trim. They are illustrated in excellent documents. They are essential to the numerous transactions, which occur at long distance in the meat trade. They are based on the efficient method in use in the packing plants to break and fabricate the meat.

Unfortunately the efficiency of high speed process does not respect the anatomy and, as a result, depreciate the whole to a lower denominator, which affects and limits, as a result, the quality, in our view, of all the industrially produced meats and sausages.

Ref: Meat Buyer's Guide, NAMP. http://www.namp.com/namp/Default.asp

Ref: Institunional Meat Specifications. http://www.ams.usda.gov/AMSv1.0/ getfile?dDocName=STELDEV3003292

PRE-CONDITIONING

A proper break down.

The proper preparation and pre-conditioning of the meat and fat are essential for the success of the further sausage processing and also for the further salting and curing of whole parts.

After slaughter the carcass is rapidly refrigerated. The temptation of the meat trade is to maintain the highest humidity to avoid shrink losses; instead, for further processing, some drying is preferable.

The pork carcass will still retain some plasticity for a day; this stage facilitates the breaking and boning operation; kept under refrigeration for a longer time the fat will further crystallize and the muscles increase rigidity. It is beneficial for the further processing, being salting or grinding and chopping.

During the first couple of days, the living muscles transform into meat. Physical and chemical reactions occur and a bacterial flora will develop on the surface of the meat. These germs are mostly innocuous; they are beneficial, even necessary factors for curing or fermenting. They play an important role in the development of the taste of the final product.

Under ancient conditions, the environment of the processing was kept dry, clean and aerated; the surfaces and containers were made of wood, having some bacteriostatic function. A flora, typical of the place, would be determining the particular flavor of the local product, like "terroir" in wine. This is why, in the past, it has been so difficult to start a "salumi" production and aim at duplicating some existing products. Today, instead, the notion of a plant flora reeks of anathema and since everybody tends to use the same starter cultures, we get uniformity of results.

The occupation of the field by a strong flora, adapted to the local conditions would make the occurrence of a massive invasion by pathogens unlikely, since the field would be occupied, but leaves open the possibility of their occasional presence at a non-contaminant level possible.

This fundamental aspect is recognized today as a directing principle of ecology; but an old paradigm of germs as dangerous, still rules the USDA system.
When I was struggling, during my first year in Fresno, California. Having to assimilate the strict requirements of the USDA for absence of pathogens in salami, I turned to "professore Cantoni dell'Università dei Studi di Milano", he is a very respected source of wisdom for the Italian "salumieri".
I clearly remember his comments... "These American are weird, they do not understand that in properly cured, fermented and dry salami, a few remaining pathogens are actually beneficial because they help to maintain the immune system active..."

Today, instead the introduction of chemical sanitation, the maintenance of high humidity in combination with vacuum packaging and mass production, offers occasional contaminants a free field if they can escape control and penetrate the products. Unfortunately, they do occasionally invade the terrain, devoid of competitors, with dire consequences.

Temperature and proper condition of the meat are critical for processing.

To understand why the conditioning of the meat is so important, we need to look at the three components of the meat and understand how to control their behavior during the different phases of the process. They are:

- Muscle fibers (myosin and actinin).
- Conjunctive tissue (mostly collagen).
- Fat tissue (fat in a collagen matrix).

In the presence of salt at a minimum of 1.5% concentration, myosin becomes soluble and forms a glue, similar to egg white; this glue is essential for the binding of the particles in a ground sausage or for the emulsion of proteins with water and fat necessary for the cohesion of sausages.

The soluble myosin coagulates at temperatures above 150°F, or if acidity drops below PH 5.5, like in the fermented products.

The soluble proteins' capacity of binding water is largely enhanced by the use of phosphate salts and the physical massage of the meat, called tumbling, which allows industrial producers to market hams (or, for that matter, beef muscle and poultry) with added water. The labeling says "natural juices", when the added water compensate the cooking loss and requires to mention "added water" for levels up to 20% above the original meat weight.

Collagen is the principal protein, forming the conjunctive tissues, like the skin and, more importantly, all the membranes and sinews holding and connecting the muscles to the bones.

Collagen has no binding capacity, but cooked in presence of water it transforms into gelatin.

The gel formed by cold gelatin, containing a variable quantity of water, which affects its firmness, binds "pâtés" and "galantines" together.

Warmed, it is the source of the juiciness of a Wiener or the lip sticking mouth-feel of a "cotechino".

Fat contained in its matrix of collagen membranes (hard fat) will retain its structure; loose fat will emulsify in a protein based mix for the good sausage, or emulsify itself the water based protein or collagen in the dreaded smearing.

Fat is present as droplets, imbedded in cells formed of conjunctive tissue. The matrix is much stronger in the layer underneath the skin. Over the neck, back and shoulders, it forms a shield. The matrix is weaker over the ham and is very soft in the crotch between the leg and the flank. Within the muscle fibers, forming the marbling of the meat, it is also abundant and very soft. Leaf lard in the abdominal cavity, the softest, is best rendered into lard.

The shield of the wild boar, armed to crash through bushes and to take the tusk wounds of competitors, is in today's pork, a layer under the skin, extending from the neck and the shoulders forward to the jowls and thinning backward all the way to the hams. It is still armed by a large quantity of collagen tissue, which forms the hard fat. It is used for the production of salami, where the fat needs to retain its original structure, distinct from the muscle.

Softer fat tissue, containing less collagen fibers, forming the marbling present between muscles in the meat, will likely bind with activated protein, collagen and water in the emulsified sausage paste.

Understanding how the combination of the different components behave together and the external conditions required to control the desired result, is essential for the mastery of the different type of sausages or meat products.

Particle definition or emulsion

To achieve the perfect separation, but good binding of the particles in salami, it is necessary to use trimmed and "de-sinewed" muscles of the shoulder, which have fine and firm fiber and fat from the hard layer of the neck and back of the pork.

When making salami, clean particle definition is essential to avoid emulsion or smearing during the grinding and blending. The lean meat is pre-cut to a size that will run through the nozzle of the grinder with a minimum of crushing. It is best refrigerated to 28°F to stiffen it and also to evaporate some of its moisture. Similarly, the fat is pre-cut and frozen to 15°F to harden and withstand the crushing of the grinder, and, then, blended with a minimum of emulsion forming during the activation of the myosin by the salt to form the paste.

Inversely, to perfect the best emulsified sausage, it is beneficial to enhance the binding capability of the muscle proteins. Pre-salting the meat as soon as possible after slaughter does it, when the higher PH of the still warm muscle will boost the solubility of the myosin.

This is why some plants break and bone the pork or the cow before refrigeration and immediately prepare the sausage or salt the still warm meat, which then can be refrigerated and maintained at a higher PH. Sausages made this way offer a better texture, color and flavor; they also will retain more water.

For precise salting and consistent results in the curing of whole meats like prosciutto it is essential to initiate the process with well rested and refrigerated meats and maintain very precise temperature in the meat and curing room.

SPICES

The vegetal realm provides us with an infinite source of herbs, roots, saps, grains, fruits, pods, bark and seeds containing compounds with aromatic, flavoring, coloring, astringent, acidifying properties and even very active bacteriostatic abilities. These are considered spices.

Nature also provides sugars, starches, proteins, emulsifiers and binders. These are considered ingredients.

This cornucopia offers vast possibilities of complementing, balancing and perfecting the natural appearance, flavor and aroma of a well made meat product. Unfortunately, it also allows to cover-up mediocre meats and process and used in excess satisfy the abused taste bud of some consumers.

I wonder how extreme distortions of the taste can occur; consider the current fad for the ever hotter spices associated with exotic labels invocating "dragon blood", "devil's", or even "inferno heat".

It is often in the simplistic, literal reliance on recipes of all kind that the apprentice errs. It is very important - I will say, fundamental - for the serious apprentice to experience and train the capacity to look, smell and taste to be able to compose the perfect symphony of taste, flavor, aroma and texture, taking into account the actual qualities of the meat and other ingredients involved in the recipe.

Feel and intuition, here, are more important than rote following.

Developing one's own sensitivity is a major aspect of the apprentice to become a creator.

Charcutier. Salumiere. Wurstmeister.

Here are some of the commonly used spices:
Pepper, nutmeg or mace, clove, cinnamon, ginger, cardamom, allspice.

Garlic, onion, chives, shallot.

Bay leaves, juniper berries.

Fennel, caraway, cumin.

Rosemary, thyme, oregano, sage, marjoram, parsley, cilantro.

Paprika, red peppers, cayenne.

Citrus, vanilla.

Hydrolyzed proteins, bouillon, aminos, soy sauce.

Learn to discriminate to evaluate the quality of spice and ingredients. The label doesn't tell or guarantee the quality of the spice; the convenience of pre-ground also opens the possibility of oxidation and venting; pre-mixes are too often mediocre.
Be careful of dosage given in recipes; spices are not standard entities with fixed values.

Take advantage of the freshness of what grows in your garden in a creative way.

I strongly feel that aiming at the best harmony each time is more important than standardizing, which inevitably sets the standard to the lowest common denominator.

Test, correct, improve… reach that unforgettable deliciousness.

INGREDIENTS

The most important, of all the possible ingredients are the minerals: salt and saltpeter as it used to be known, potassium nitrate nowadays, but mostly used as "pink salt", sodium nitrate and sodium nitrite.

Salt

As in "Salzgut", "salumi", "salaisons" it is the key element able to transform and preserve meats. Sodium chloride has been used for millennia to preserve and flavor, it is available in many forms, more or less refined. The rock salt or sea salt which, can also contain traces of many other minerals, is to be preferred. A fine tongue can distinguish nuances from one type of salt from another and be able to choose the best tasting.

- Salt draws water from the proteins; it hampers bacterial life, acts as a preservative.

- Salt renders the muscle proteins, myosin and actinin, soluble. This effect is central to the capacity of meat, (muscle, collagen and fat) to bind. All the meat products processed with salt depend on this phenomenon to hold together.

- The action of the salt depends of the state of the muscle. Immediately after slaughter, when the carcass is still warm, the muscle PH (6.5) is still relatively high and the muscle proteins with the addition of salt will form a stronger binding; stronger binding results in better texture and taste in the products.

- Modern science has found a way to raise the PH of cold muscle (5.8) with the application of calcium polyphosphate. Per se, a good thing, because it is a valuable nutrient; unfortunately, it also allows for the use of tired or lesser quality meats and has led to the habit of pumping-up salted and cooked meats with added water.

The understanding of how to develop the binding, how to consolidate it with its coagulation by cooking or acidifying, is a key for the mastery of meat products.

Every comminuting sausage technique will produce some emulsion of the components, binding together muscle, fat, collagen and water.

The complete transformation by emulsion occurs in those products where, the whole material is emulsified, where the original texture of the components disappears, transformed in a totally different texture.

With salami, instead, where ideally, the particles of muscle and fat will bind together with the least emulsion, it cannot be totally avoided. It happens during the grinding, blending and stuffing, due to the rubbing mechanical process.

Blending, in different proportions, whole particles of meat and emulsified paste allows for a great variation of products with a great variation of textures.

The emulsion is part of the process but needs to be stabilized by coagulation for the finished product. There are different ways to obtain the desired result. It is the basis to the different categories of products.

With their sense of organization and method, the Germanic "Wurstmeister" distinguishes the **"Brühwurst"** (poached), the **"Kochwust"** (cooked) and the **"Rohwurst"** (raw, fermented). Hot or cold smoking usually complements the treatments.

To set the emulsion, either temperature above 150 °F will coagulate the proteins, (the higher proportion of soluble myosin and actinin, the firmer the coagulated emulsion), or the acidification resulting from the fermentation at low temperature will set. The quality of the setting defines the mouth-feel of the final product.

The salt concentration is measured in proportion to the total weight of the meat and added ingredients. (It is very important to respect this proportion, while making emulsified paste when adding significant proportions of ice, water or milk).

The salt per cent concentration target for the product has to be adjusted in function of processing; whatever loss is occurring has to be compensated. For example, while dry curing a whole muscle with salt, rubbing lasts several days, the concentration target consists of the fraction of the added salt, which penetrates the meat by osmosis, rather than, the fraction eliminated as brine, which is discarded. The salt percent weighed for this process must cover both the proportions penetrating the meat and lost with the brine.

In practice about a third of the salt will be eliminated with the brine formed during a two week salting of a piece of meat like a five pound CT butt for "coppa".

In the recipes we indicate the total percentage of salt to be used, it includes the anticipated loss. The small quantity of the curing agent is added on top.

- Simple cooked products require about 1% of salt.
- For the proper development of the protein binding, sausage require a minimum of **1.5%** of salt.
- Salami and dry cured meats require at least **2.5%** of salt since they rely on the salt concentration to control the bacterial flora during curing and fermenting. Interestingly, this higher concentration of salt, which will increase with the drying of the product, is not overbearing since part of this added salt binds to the proteins during aging and, as such, does not affect the taste buds.

Saltpeter

The ancient designation of potassium nitrate is the traditional and still preferred curing agent in combination with salt and a small quantity of sugar. The natural curing process implies bacterial activity and time. In faster modern techniques it can be replaced, directly with nitrite of sodium, acting without the intervention of the curing flora. The modern shortcut, though, is lacking in aroma and flavor. There is nothing like the good old saltpeter, bacteria and time for quality.

Sugar

It can be used in its many forms, from honey to corn syrup; besides sweetening, it is needed in small quantities in the order of 0.5% to support the beneficial activity of the fermenting bacteria during the curing of the meats. It is possible, at least in chemical theory, to control the degree of acidification in salami making, with the quantity and composition of sugars.

This is where finesse replaces theory, since the process is also depending on the time – temperature, the natural sugar (glycogen) content of the meat and the texture and quality of the paste.

Wine

Sometime cider or beer, is a frequent and beneficial addition to many products; a variety is added bringing a different proportion, of alcohol, sugar, acidity and aroma.

Phosphate

These salts are commonly used to enhance the capacity of meats to bind and retain water; they raise the PH of the proteins, thus increasing their capacity to bind to water. This technique associated to tumbling or massage of the meat is commonly used to improve the yield and, to speed up production. To further increase yield, the usage of extenders like starches, corn syrup, the flour of seeds like mustard, external proteins from soy, whey or milk, are added.

Water

The addition of water has an obvious purpose to increase the volume of the meat and lower the cost; but it decreases the nutritional value of the final product. It may be a beneficial factor in order to increase the juiciness or to achieve a more delicate structure; but it increases the perishability.

The chemistry of food additives is very extensive and sophisticated, their control and regulation never catching up with the creativity of the chemical industry. We need to be aware of its existence and keep our distance.

Extenders, binders, emulsifiers, colorants, artificial flavorings and bacteriological stabilizers are available. They are not needed to work with quality meats for outstanding results.

No need to artificially extend shelf life, better to respect freshness.

Some traditional ingredients have a specific usage:

Milk is used as the emulsifying liquid in sausages like the Swiss "Kalbsbratwurst".

Gelatin or aspic is used to moisten, bind and garnish "Pâtés".

Skin Block ("Schwartenblock") helps in the binding and gives juiciness to the sausage. It is part of the recipe of many emulsified German sausages; usually it is used at the rate of 10-20%. It is produced raw from pre-salted skin, ground and emulsified, or from pre-cooked skins. The skin collagen thus comminuted, transforms into gelatin when the sausage is cooked.

Potatoes, pre-cooked, even fish like anchovies, are used as ingredient of some Scandinavian sausages.

Bread is part of the British bangers.

Cheese is used in some variety Hot-Dogs.

Cabbage, pre-cooked is the key in the Swiss "saucisse aux choux".

The list will extend in function of the scope of your creativity, but will hit the restrictions imposed by inspection.

Note that the ingredients have to be listed in order of decreasing importance on the label. USDA uses the approval procedure of the label to keep track of all authorized ingredients.

Starter Cultures have to be listed as ingredients for the fermenting sausages. **Molds and Yeast** instead, applied outside the casing, do not need to be mentioned as ingredients on the label probably because, in theory, they will be eliminated with the casing though they participate in the meat maturation.

SALTING

Speck Tirolese in the salt

Salt is the core ingredient of the trade. The application of the salt and cure to the meats is the decisive operation. A seasoned steak or hamburger is no sausage; but at a certain threshold and with time and proper handling, involving bacterial, enzymatic and other processes, salting is what makes sausage.

Methods and quantity vary, our modern palate, luckily more sensitive, demands less salt than what was the norm in more rustic conditions. The hygiene of modern meat production also allow for salt levels, which would have been considered risky in the past.

Dry salting prosciutto

Sea salt alone applied at the rate of 3 – 4 % to prosciutto is spread in a coarse form over the leg, to dissolve slowly in the relatively dry and cold environment of the salting cellar. The process is repeated a couple of times, preceded by a thorough massage of the leg to help the penetration. The active salting last about 3 weeks for a large leg, followed by a month of rest, allowing for the drying of the surface and the osmotic equalization of the salt throughout the meat. About 2 to 2.5 % of salt will be absorbed during the whole process.

Prosciutto and other meats can be treated with salt alone, if allowed to age for a very long time - more than a full year as a rule. This requires, of course, a particular method to limit the drying to about a third of the initial weight. "Stucco" applied at that stage, protects the prosciutto from excess drying.

The meat reaching a salt concentration of 4% becomes sterile.

The enzymatic maturation during the long aging stabilizes red pigments in the meat in a way similar to how the nitrate reduction does in full curing over a shorter period of time.

Before you get involved here, you need to review the chapter about **CURING.**

Dry salting "coppa", etc.

Smaller meat cuts, like the "coppa", loin, boneless ham and belly, can be salted with the nitrate cure in similar fashion using the dry ingredients, salt, cure and sugar with spices, weighed at 2.5 – 3 % of the raw meat weight; the meat and ingredients are rubbed in, then let rest under refrigeration for a few days, the meat rotated and rubbed again until ready. At least 3-4 days are needed for thin meats like belly or lighter cuts, up to two weeks for heavy and thick pieces like boneless ham.

The brine produced is then discarded and the meat let to equalize for a repeated length of time.

Equalizing is the time allowed, without additional salt, for the full penetration throughout the meat. It is very important for meats, which are protected on one side, like the "speck Tirolese" by fat and skin, which prevent the penetration of the salt.

The process can be helped with starter culture; they assist the reduction of nitrate, will fight unwanted germs like listeria and contribute to the development of flavor.

Dry salting for cooking

Old fashion Ham salting for cooking uses the same method, but with less salt to absorb only 1.5% in the meat. From a total 2-2.5%, this slow salting method allows for the natural growth and action of halophile bacteria, similar to the ones fermenting salami. The lacto bacterial activity helps the curing and develops that old true flavor of ham, which the modern injection process cannot achieve and is commonly replaced with all kinds of added flavorings.

Brining

The classic salting implies immersion in brine. It is convenient to quickly salt the heads destined for the production of headcheese. Use basic brine at 10% of salt and cure, 0.5% of sugar and some spice. Adding proper starters to the brine will help the curing process. The timing/temperature of brining is important to determine the quantity of salt that the meat will absorb.

Fancy decoctions of spices or herbs allow for brine functioning also as a marinade.

Pre-cooking the brine seems, in my experience, not useful, unless it is meant for injection. And even then I doubt the sterility of the process.

The industrial production process shortens the curing time to a minimal overnight cycle. Salt, cure, other ingredients and flavoring are **injected as brine** to a volume of 10%, up to more than 30%, at corresponding concentrations of salt, and then massaged in tumbler, under vacuum and temperature control, to be absorbed in the meat.

1.5% of salt is the trigger level for the activation of the protein in order to get the binding that will make sausages.

2.5 % of salt is the minimum safe level for the curing and fermenting of Salami and other Dry Cured Sausages that will be dried, possibly smoked and consumed without cooking.

There are, of course, exceptions, like the "saucisson" of eastern France and Switzerland, made of selected meats and fat coarsely ground, at 1.5% of salt and cured with some white wine or a pinch of sugar, but no water, which are partially dried (10-15%), smoked with a slight fermentation during the process. They will keep for weeks and are usually served cooked. Some can be further dried and be eaten as dry sausage.

CHOPPING

The Bowl Chopper, Buffalo chopper or Cutter, called "Blitz" in German, is the typical sausage-making machine.

It can be used to pre-mince and possibly mix meats, in preparation for grinding; or it can generate any kind of textures all the way to the finest emulsions.

Several knives mounted on a shaft, rotate at adjustable speeds transversally to the bowl shaped like an open donut, which turns and brings the meat around to the knives. At low speed the knives only cut; if the bowl rotates, relatively, faster than the knives, the blades act like the pallets of a blender. At very high speed the knives become extremely noisy, ultra-sonic shock waves are created, the mechanical action contributes to the perfection of emulsion.

In the small kitchen, blenders like Cuisinart or Robot-Coupe offer the same function as the bowl chopper. The French like to use the larger Stefan cutter, which is based on the same principle: open bowl with a rotating blade at the bottom center, which cuts and stirs the paste. The pre-conditioning of the meats, according to their type, is very important factor to achieve the desired result. Just slightly frozen and still plastic for the lean; fat stiff frozen but yielding to the knife is how best results can be achieved.

Coarse "nostrano" salami paste.

97

Salami

The purpose is to achieve a paste with segregated particles of lean and fat, sufficiently blended and cohesive to be stuffed. Meat and fat can be introduced together in the bowl, slightly frozen, the coldest for the finest texture to limit melting and the forming of emulsion.

When particles reach the desired size, and when their temperature rises, due to the action of the knives, add the salt and ingredients, including the starters and the wine, and switch to the mixing phase. Anticipate that the particle size will still be reduced somewhat during mixing.

Note that salt added to ice, still present in the muscle as small crystals, will melt the ice and drop the temperature. The final temperature should be high enough to allow for the development of the binding capability of the protein, but low enough to allow stuffing without smearing.

I often observe whole carts of paste becoming a solid frozen block, difficult or impossible to stuff, when the meat and fat were brought too cold to the chopper. The process of cutting and mixing was going apparently OK, but the paste freezes a few minutes later because of the reaction to the salt. It then takes quite a long time to raise the temperature of the block to be able to stuff it.

The whole process of cutting and mixing without emulsion requires a limited number of cutting knives, usually four, spinning only at the lower speed.

It is possible to control the relative size of the particles of fat and meat, for instance in chopping first the fat to reduce its size. It is very important in this case to insure the clean cutting of the fat and avoid crushing it, which would lead to smearing. It is helpful to add some lean to "lubricate" the slicing action of the knives.

When making a paste for salami with the cutter, often the mixing is not sufficient and the paste benefits from resting in the cooler for a day or two before stuffing. It is beneficial in several ways: the salt equalizes, the myosin gets tacky and the binding improves, the curing develops with the growth of the ferments, the texture and flavor benefit.

Paste for a Saucisson de Lyon.

Sausage

A plain texture at different degree of coarseness can be achieved. Clean meat and hardest fat allow for the coarsest paste.

Start with meats and fat, just slightly stiffened by frost, add the salt and ingredients early in the process to develop binding during the comminuting phase.

Use only low speeds for the whole process.

The mechanical cutting will generate emulsion. The proportion of emulsion from minimal with coarse paste to eventual total transformation, will define the nature, type and texture of the sausage.

The energy spent during the cutting is heating the paste. Keep it under control with the addition of ice chips or start with colder meats. Be aware though that you will develop the best binding, hence, best texture of the sausage, at a temperature of about 50° F.

A common technique consists of adding meats at different stages to achieve more complex texture. Start the process with an emulsified paste, "marked" later with coarser meat, which should be pre-salted, if the size of the particles is to stay big. (This is the way to make a Polish "kielbasa" with big cured ham pieces bound by a fine emulsion).

Emulsion

The cutter needs to be outfitted with the full set of emulsifying knives and operated at highest speed. Ice is added to control the temperature, which will be raised during the process to facilitate the formation of the emulsion and to achieve the perfect plasticity of the paste for stuffing.

A proven method is to begin a first phase with the lean meat only, best lightly frozen, adding immediately all the salt and cure.

During the initial chopping, add half the intended flaked ice (10%). When the temperature reaches +6°C, a very strong emulsification of the lean with water and salt will form. Due to the soluble myosin the paste will become very tacky and, becomes able during the second phase of the process to absorb the fat and more ice. At this point the emulsion is in a water-phase, protein and salt with inclusion of the little fat that came with the meat.

This point in the process is reached, determined by the formation of a smooth very sticky paste and the temperature raising to +6°C. Use your hand to help the mixing in the bowl and feel the progressive transformation until the sticky mass holds from your hand and becomes hard to shake down.

The emulsion has to be strong enough to now absorb progressively the fat and the rest of the ice (10%) or other liquid, like milk or broth, the spices, and eventual starters. Keep chopping at high speed until the temperature reaches 10-12°C. (The critical temperature to get the most activation of the protein binding).

The strength of the emulsion will condition the "bite" or 'knack" of the sausage.

The paste can be stuffed immediately or refrigerated for later use.

If the quality of the ingredients or the process is poorly mastered, there is a risk to invert the emulsion into a fat phase with inclusion of water-proteins. The feared smearing of the paste! This would mean the end of the project, though there are ways to revert the paste *(the French would say "ratrapper")*. You could use strong binders like NFDM (non fat dry milk) and liquid to reverse the emulsion.

Skin Block

A different type of paste can be produced from pork skin, composed nearly exclusively of collagen. Skin, cleaned free of fat are pre salted; this will make them absorb moisture and somewhat soften them. They need to be ground in several steps, starting with the grinding plate with the largest hole, like 1" down to ¼" or less. It can be done with several plates and knives mounted in a very strong grinder, or successive grinding with diminishing plate size. The chopper will reduce the fibers into a paste with the addition of 10-20% of ice. The thick slurry will set in container under refrigeration.

An alternative method is, to first cook the skins, which will be easier to comminute into a paste, using less water.

When set after refrigeration, the block of skin can be cut in rubbery chunks and incorporated as an ingredient to sausage (best to grind down the skin block, with the meats to facilitate the incorporation into the paste). Its role is to extend the gel of the emulsion, with more collagen, which will transform into gelatin, at cooking temperature, adding juiciness to the sausage.

"Pâté de champagne".

"Pâtés" and "Mousses"

France and Belgium are the source of a whole category of products, always cooked or baked in crocks and molds, but also incorporated in pastry.

Meat Pies

They have a more British accent. Requiring the skill of the pastry chef.

"Fleishkaese" or Meatloaves

Germanic creations, They are composed of fully emulsified paste., sometime including a "marking". In America's cuisine the relatives of the "Fleischkaese" are the popular meatloaves.

The cutter is the tool of choice for the preparation of these different pastes.

"Fleischkaese" *(to confuse you, the French call that "fromage d'Italie")* are simple meat and fat emulsion, which can include a small proportion of liver.

"Pâtés" are a coarse blend of meat ad fat, with inclusion of organs like liver, demanding the addition of binders like egg or lacto-proteins. They are worked, cold in the cutter at low speed, cut to the desired particle size, then blended.

"Mousses" are processed hot, starting with hot, parboiled soft fat (typically the trimming of the ham, called "mouilles" in French). They are chopped down in a cream, milk, broth or gelatin, with an emulsifier and salt, cure and spices. When the warm fat-phase emulsion is done, the cold liver, which has been previously pureed, and, possibly, other organs or meats are incorporated.

The resulting warm paste is immediately stuffed or put in molds for further baking.

"Pâtés de campagne" or "pâtés en croute", often combine, pre-marinated meats and different types of paste.

The pride of innovation.

GRINDING

Who knows, by who and where this most ancient machine was invented?
We all have seen old, hand-cranked, cast iron antiques in gran'pa's kitchen.
Modern ones can be big and complex, powerful machines, offering sophistication
like differential rotation speed for screw and blade. Most have a mixing bowl hop-
per to feed the screw of the grinder.

The grinder works on a different principle, no fast cutting blades, but the screw in it's housing advances and pushes up to a high pressure, the meats into the rotating knife, gliding in front of the perforated plate. The caliber of the plates holes determine the particle size of the paste and the future look of the slice of the salami or sausage, which will differ by its uniformity from those made with the cutter.

Velati's grinder-mixer.

The scissor-like comminuting effect of the knife and plate under high pressure affects the texture of the meat, which will bind more easily to form the paste. Best grinders have a short nozzle with helicoïdal ridges oriented across the edge of the screw . Those built with straight ridges don't seem to work well.

There is an obvious difference in the texture of both pastes made at the same particle size, with grinder or cutter.

The mechanical action of the grinder creates the risk of crushing the fat instead of cutting; this is the main cause of paste smear, turning all or part of the lean and fat into an undesirable fat-phase emulsion; this needs to be absolutely avoided for the production of salami and possibly tolerated for most of the coarse sausages, when the further mixing will reverse it. Instead, it is a desirable form, in some kind of breakfast sausages or spreadable "salame" like the spreadable "nduja" or "sobrasada".

To control smearing, knife and plate need to be sharp and perfectly matched. The selection of the meat and fat is also very important. For the best salami, the clean trimmed meats must be slightly frozen (28°F) and reduced in size to flow easily through the nozzle and screw of the grinder; the hard fat must be frozen at a lower temperature (15-20°F) and reduced in size by clean cutting, avoiding any crushing.

The clean grinding effect is improved by pre-mixing and running lean and fat together.

Pay extreme attention to the feeding of the grinder screw, making sure that the meat and fat are carried forward and ground, without back flush, which turns the screw into a mixing and blending machine producing the unwanted smear. Also control the outflow to verify that meat and fat come out clean.

Easily hard sinews or bone particles can create a space between knife and plate that will prevent the clean cutting action. Immediately stop grinding and clean thoroughly knife and plate before resuming,

Some grinders are equipped with plates having a helicoïdal gutter that will collect bone particles or sinews and push them through a separate outlet at the center of the plate to be discarded.

Grinder is also the traditional tool of choice for the preparation of the "mortadella" paste. The meats are solid frozen, usually pre-flaked and run through a succession of grinder knives and plates of reducing caliber, down to a 1 mm size. The extreme crushing and comminuting readies the resulting paste for an ulterior' energetic mixing, where pre-washed "lardelli" are added with salt spices and other ingredients. This way a paste can be prepared without the need for much water in the form of ice to control the temperature.

Less water in the paste and evaporation during the oven-baking, will yield a dense "mortadella" with a long shelf life.

Contrary to the chopping process, which limits the batch size to the contents of one chopping bowl, the grinding can be continuous and limited only by the size of the dedicated blender.

Chopping, Blending, Stuffing machine.

MIXING, BLENDING, BINDING

I frequently use the term blending instead of mixin; this comes from the common designation in the industry of large blenders, which we should be calling mixers.

Well mixed
Saucissons de Lyon.

Mixers of different size and function exist; the more sophisticated are equipped with vacuum and refrigeration, even programming phases.

Mixing is an essential stage in the production of sausages or salami. The first function is to blend ingredients into the meat, unless this was done before grinding or during the chopper processing. The second, very critical function is to activate the myosin (the red muscle fiber protein), which in the presence of salt (at least 1.5% concentration), becomes soluble, forming a glue, which will bind the paste and hold the sausage together when coagulated by cooking or fermentation.

In the presence of activated protein, the mixing can also form emulsion, which will be undesirable in the salami, but needed in some sausage, when the emulsion is of the proper kind - water-phase emulsion of fat in protein and water. The reverse, smear, leads to failed products.

Basic mixing can be done by hand for small batches of sausages or salami. Take the precaution to avoid warming up the paste. A salami paste, which needs to retain its particle definition, will be mixed with open fingers, with a raking effect, to blend the ingredients; this is helped by the lubrication effect of some wine. As a result, when the salt activates the protein and when the blend becomes sticky, the paste is packed together by the pressure of the flat hands.

For sausage, the most efficient way is to crush the paste in closing fingers over a handful and to punch the paste until if forms a sticky, homogenous mass.

ACTIVATION OF THE PROTEIN AND EMULSIFYING
FULL UNDERSTANDING OF THE ROLE OF ACTIVATED PROTEINS IS AT THE CORE OF THE ART OF SAUSAGE.

In my opinion, this is the most important aspect of the craft. It has to be fully understood and, more, it has to be felt and seen. The emulsion we need is water-based. It is formed by water, which is bound with the active, soluble, proteins of the muscle; it is not the reverse oil-based one. This one to us is smear, though it is what you do, when you do stir a mayonnaise.

Any meat paste will tend, or "prefer" to go water-based, but overstressed, it will reverse.

The process is exploited to its maximum when making fully emulsified paste, but the understanding and the application of the principle will mean success or failure when making any sausage and not least salami.

Let me attempt to explain:

- *The amount of water-based "glue" is limited by the type and composition of a paste.*

- *Enough glue is needed to wrap around and absorb all the particles of fat. It is one thing to "glue" large particles of fat in a coarse salami paste and may be impossible without smearing, to reduce the size of the particles to achieve a fine paste, without added liquid.*

- *In the chopper work, we add water in the form of ice to keep the paste cool and more importantly, to extend the liquid phase to become able to fully absorb the fat in a 100% emulsified paste.*

- *Water-based bound paste will set or coagulate with fermentation or cooking.*

- *Fat-based, smeared paste will break and never bind; but it is reversible; a strong binder, like non-fat dry milk powder and more water, or a natural glue-like egg white, could salvage, otherwise, lost material.*

We rely on the chemistry of two proteins - myosin and actinin, which salt partially transforms in a kind of glue, (similar to egg white) which will absorb water and will emulsify fat. This combination will also absorb gelatin formed from collagen.

Different proportions of the paste components bound by that "glue", will have different textures, different qualities. These infinite variations are infinite potential for the creative craftsman.

Some form of mixing is necessary to activate the proteins.

Full-blended, emulsified proteins and fat completely alter the matrix and texture of the originals components. The natural barrier formed by the membranes of the muscles and the fat tissue are broken; water is added and the result forms a type of gel, where all the components interact intimately, actually transforming the substance. This is the cause of the difference in the structure of a hot dog and salami.

Emulsions take two forms: the desirable one consists of absorbing the fat as micro particles into a liquid and protein phase. This type of emulsion will coagulate with heat or acidification and yield a smooth gel, resulting in a clean mouth-feel. The alternative, where oil phase is absorbing particles of water and protein, is the dreaded smear, though some spreadable products are based on this reversed type of emulsion.

In its simplest form, when making salami, activated proteins are binding meat and fat particle without forming any emulsion, it is the ideal condition for success. It will form the perfect medium in which the fermentation can take place; as a result acidification coagulates the soluble proteins to set the salami.

Proper binding also creates the ideal conditions for the enzymatic maturation and facilitates the drying.

In real life, it is difficult to create the perfect conditions for binding without at least some emulsion. It can be done when working a small batch exclusively with knife and hands. The machines, grinder, mixer, stuffer - because of friction - will always yield some emulsion or smear.

The relative proportion of particles to emulsion defines the many types of products.

The quality is also influenced by the proportions of muscle proteins, collagen, fat and water.

The body of a sausage is defined by the strength of the emulsion. It provides for the proper binding between the sausage paste and the casing necessary for smoking.

In the case of emulsion, cooking sets the paste, transforming it into the sausage.

CASINGS

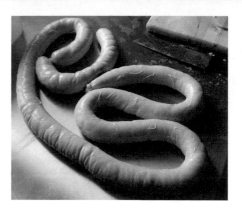

Kalbsbratwurst in pork middle.

Beef middle.

Beef bung.

The paste or the whole muscle needs to be contained and protected from the environment, but it still needs to evaporate or breathe in a certain way; it needs to absorb smoke or support the growth of beneficial molds and yeasts. To insure these functions, the casing needs to become part of the product, binding to it.

Traditionally, the resource exists in the animal intestine, which offers tubes and pouches, with a perfect affinity for the meats. Guts come in two types: small intestine - very long, curved, regular in shape, lean, with only one layer of fibers; large intestine - shorter, more complex in shape, from the caecum to the rectum, fatter, with multiple layers of fibers.

Stomach, bladder and caecum form bigger pouches for large sausages and whole dry cured meats like the "culatello", which is set in a bladder after salting.

Guts from the small intestine of sheep, pork and beef, called middles, are used for sausages and salami of small size. They are very permeable and will dry rapidly. Coming in long section they are convenient to stuff and portion. Being mechanically cleaned, they are readily available and cheaper than the hand processed large intestines.

They exist also as re-manufactured casings, produced by cutting and sewing for larger shape, sometime doubling the layers for large, long-aging salami.

Pasted casings ("incollati") are stuffing ready, individual, dry tubes, manufactured by gluing over a mold, the open cut sections of pork middle.

Large intestine like beef bungs are curved, large casing for traditional large salami, or big sausages like "salame cotto" or "mortadella"; they are also very convenient to cover dry-cured cuts like "coppa" and "lonzo".

Pork large intestine, are called chitterling in the US, they are the casing of choice for sausage and salami meant to age more slowly and gain aroma from the casing itself. More difficult to clean by hand, they cannot be used as sold in bulk by packers. Most originate in China, where they are cleaned, calibrated, cut to size and pre-tied. In this country they are less available, only from some specialized casing providers and they can be quite expensive. They demand more skill to handle, are slower to fill and more difficult to bind, but they confer class and add quality to the products.

Europeans love their best dry sausages like "salame Felino", "rosette de Lyon", "salchichon de Vich", stuffed in the pork rectum - thickest and fattest of all casings. In French, "rosette" is the elegant nickname of what we call ass-hole. The Italians call, more matter of factly, the same "budello culare". The long straight section from the "culare" including the "filzetta", before the bulges of the "crespone" (chitterling) is called "budello gentile". Gentle, because it cares delicately for the salami.

Modern industrial casings supplement the naturals. They are made of different materials. Closest to the intestines are collagen casings made of extruded collagen paste and tanned like leather with acids from the smoke. The collagen casings exist in all shapes and function, even edible small caliber used for breakfast sausages or hot dogs. Their permeability and their protein origin are closest to small intestines.

Collagen is also extruded in thin film, called "cofi film", convenient to cover and protect whole muscle after salting to protect them during fermenting and aging, as an alternative to natural bung or bladder.

Fibrous casings are made from a paper made of hemp fibers, coated with collagen to insure binding and permeability. The fibrous casings, being essentially cellulose, can be destroyed by too much mold and yeast growing on the salami. The penicillia molds are wood decaying fungus able to digest cellulose!

Cellophane was used to form water permeable casing for cooked sausages, it is still in use in Italy, shaped in multi layered pouches, used to hold up to several hundred pounds of paste for the "mortadella gigante", which will cook for days.

All kind of watertight plastic casings are available for cooked sausages, replacing stitched casings in products like the "Braunschweiger" liver sausage.

Today after the mad cow disease scare, mostly pork and sheep casings are used. The Italian still use the excellent horse casing for their renown "salame di Milano"; it keeps perfect shape, ages well and is easy to peel; not so, the pork casing, whose protein bind solidly to their kin's meat.

Small intestine (pork middles) come in "hanks" or bundle, calibrated, sufficient to stuff 100 Lbs. of paste. They are very long, regular in shape, only the gut muscle fiber layer is left. The food contents are flushed and then the internal mucous tissue is removed. The storage in abundant salt hardens the fiber and eliminates all the germs.

The large intestine, much shorter, is very irregular, beginning with a big pouch then progressively narrowing, first with big side bulges - that's the chitterling, "crespone" in Italy, "chaudin" in France; then, it becomes a regular tube, "filzetta" in Italy and ends up named after, "la rosette" des Français, or "il culare" in Italy.

"Crespone or chaudin", (pork chitterlings).

The large intestine consists of a double-muscular fiber hull, with a thin, fatty tissue in-between. This structure is less permeable and slows down the drying process, which confers a unique aroma to the salami.

All natural casings, kept in heavy salt, need pre-rinsing and flushing before use. The large intestines are used inside out, which sometimes hides inside, the un-sufficiently trimmed connecting tissues and adhering fat.

Artificial casings are made tough, to be mechanically portioned and clipped. Natural casings, instead, need to be hand tied. Some machines exist that reproduce hand tying with twine for small salami.

Twisting alternately is also a way to portion small casings.

Most casings are peeled before consumption or slicing. Pork middles and sheep casing are usually eaten with the product.

Sometimes it helps to moisten the casing of salami, which has gotten too dry, in order to ease the peeling.

Hand stuffing "mortadella di fegato".

STUFFING

Introducing the paste or the muscle into the chosen container or casing is a cumbersome task. The nature and consistency of the paste make it a tricky job, barely possible, just using the hands. The job is facilitated by a tube funnel, which we call a horn, over which the tubular casing can be pulled. The paste is pumped through the horn into the casing by the stuffer.

Some do it for home production using the grinder screw, mounted with a horn instead of a knife and blade. This system is very slow and greatly increases the risk of smearing.

Small, hand cranked stuffers make a small job easier.

Modern equipment transfers the charges of paste via standard wagons, which are mechanically loaded into the stuffer hopper. A slowly rotating screw bring the paste down into a dual pump, the main pump pushes mechanically the paste into the stuffing horn; another, a vacuum pump, removes the air from the paste to improve its density and consistency.

With the old hydraulic or electric stuffer, the operator controlled the speed, the stop and go motion of the stuffer, using his leg to control the function while holding the casing with one hand on the horn, acting as a brake, in order to control the pressure of the paste into the casing and shaping sausage with the other hand by pinching the casing, at length, where it is meant to be twisted or tied.

Controlling the pressure of the paste in the casing is a difficult thing to do and it has a great impact on the following job to portion the sausage on the table, be it by twisting or by twine binding.

Doing all of that with the hand crank stuffer, a single operator mastering all the functions with only two hands is as masterful as playing Paganini on the fiddle!

Now the vacuum stuffer is electronically controlled and the nature of the job changes to learn how to set the parameters on a touch screen. These machines offer all kind of functions, like:

- Multiple barrels to load casing over the horn while stuffing with the other.
- Adjustable brake controlling the release of the casing and, thus, the pressure.

- Mechanical loading of the natural casing on the horn.
- Portion and twist while stuffing.

There is even the possibility of installing a grinding knife and plate at the head of the horn to re-calibrate a paste.

The portioning of the casing can also be done by machine; different type of clippers can be fitted to the stuffer and synchronized via computer link. They use stronger artificial casings and can produce strings of linked sausages, separated by a single or double clip; they can also clip long and bigger chubs at both ends, adding a loop for rack hanging.

There exists an Italian machine, which can tie with twine small natural or collagen casing into "cacciatori' or "salametti"; but with most natural casings it is still the job of the craftsman to hand tie.

INJECTING AND TUMBLING (DEVIL'S WORK)

Half a century ago, pumps feeding with brine racks of injecting needles were developed, to pump brine into the meat. It would save time for curing. It happened at the time of the discovery of the phosphates propriety to increase the protein retention of water. It was easy to replace the natural aromas and flavor deriving from enzymes work, during the slow curing, with spices and flavorings. Tumbling replaced the slow action of natural curing. The door to "improved productivity = lesser quality" was open.

Speed and profit were irresistible and consumers had to get used to soft moist cooked meats.

The technique, which started with injecting whole legs through the blood vessels, evolved into a new industry creating, ever-improved injectors and tumblers.

Nowadays, the meat is prepared, slashed and peeled from the membranes to expose the muscle proteins; it is then injected on a conveyor passing under multiple needles to pump at regulated pressure the complex brine mixtures in the meat. The bloated meat is then dumped into tumblers, not unlike the modern washing machine, which will massage and rest through cycles of vacuum and release. The proteins activate and transform until they form a glue, which will hold the parts together when cooked after stuffing.

Of course, this method took the industry into very dangerous territory, since the addition of water into the core and massaging expands exponentially the potential for germ growing.

The volume of water and extenders of all kinds - milk, soy, egg or blood proteins - allow to transform natural muscles into "Jello" like compounds. The State had to regulate the products to keep the industry under control.

Lunch and common deli meat today contain from 10 to 30% added liquid.

Such products, with high water content, have to be sliced and packaged for longer shelf life, required by the distributor and the grocer. With their high water content they are, highly perishable. To control pathogens the industry has evolved into a germ-obsessed activity of ultimate refrigeration, processing controls, use of preservatives, pasteurizing, extreme sanitizing, slicing and packaging requiring operating room-like procedures, with lab support.

Fighting life has replaced the balance of natural processes. Quality got lost on the way.

TWINE AND NETS

To tie efficiently, it is good to use a hemp twine, spooled around a short dowel fitting in the hand. The twine is pre-soaked to slide over the casing in order to be positioned for the knot while the free hand pinches the casing. The wet hemp twine retains its strength; it glides easily over the shaping slippery sausage and still it will lock itself in a single or double key and won't loosen up.

The caliber of the twine has to be matching the size of the piece to be tied; it is good to have two or three sizes handy. It was available everywhere, when "macramé" was fashionable. Today it can be found relatively easily in the Internet, while butcher suppliers are still offering only cotton twine.

It is well known in the trade, that cotton or worst synthetic twine has driven "salum-ieri" totally "nuts" (The author is speaking for himself here). Either they don't slide and impede the process, or they loosen at the worst time, causing disaster.

Large salami are usually bridled, lengthwise and cross wise to hold their weight and compress the paste as much as possible for the dripping phase; anticipating that with the paste drying, the twine will get loose.

Nets can replace the complex tying in order to hang the sausage of greater bulk for further smoking, cooking or fermenting. "stockinettes" are made of loose, shape-fitting cotton netting; they are very handy to hang odd shaped bone in meats. Nets with or without elastic, even woven of plastic, can be used to support heavy pieces.

TYING

Binding the "mortadella di fegato"

To bind chains of "cacciatori", it takes nimble fingers and flexible wrists to pass the spool around the casing and a firm bicep pull, to get the knotting tight, then a gentle stretch to tense the running length of the twine that will hold the weight of the sausages in a chain. The motion repeats itself for twelve times, if that's the number of units on the chain. A loop on each end, will allow hanging the chain on the stick for the fermenting and drying.

The advantage of the hemp twine is that it will hold in place over the casing with a single knot. Coming from the previous knot, the twine spool is held in the right hand and stretched alongside the next salami lying on the table. The left pulls the twine underneath and over the salami, gliding the loose end under the casing in the knotting position. The right then passes the spool under the twine held by the left, forming the knot, which is pulled tight by the right hand, first in a movement to create the tension on the string, between knots, to support the weight of the chain of salami, and then positioning and tightening the knot, leveraging with the spool held in hand….

I hope you get it, It is amazing to experience how difficult it is for most to get the flow of the movement, I must have shown it, and will do it again hundreds of times; then there is the forming and tightening of the loop… but that is another story! I'll show you when we meet.

Learning to tie in the different modes is achieved when the hands can do it automatically without thinking. Some serious training is required to become efficient with twine, spool in hand and achieve consistent, well-formed individual salamis or chains.

Larger chubs will be supported by twine running the length of the casing, secured by belting at intervals and a strong loop formed for hanging. Depending on the size and style, the number of length and cross loops can increase, to end looking like a netting.

This kind of containment by twine becomes quite artful, when tying the "culatello". It is more like knitting a tight shirt over the body; It has to allow for further tightening after the initial drying.

It demands a strong team of operators, with heavy twine or outright rope, to tie a giant "mortadella" weighing 200 lb. or more.

CURING

Curing is a transforming process, which modifies certain aspects and properties of the meat and is essential to preserve, improve the taste and texture of all sausages and other meat products. The term actually implies a double process salting and nitrate reduction.

It can be done in a few cases by salt alone, like for fresh sausages, with a limited shelf life; or, at the other extreme, for very long-aging "prosciutto", in which case the modifications in texture, taste and color are the result of slow enzymatic processes.

Complete curing combines **salt, sugar, saltpeter and microorganisms** - respectively about 2% salt of the total meat, 0.5% sugar, 0.03% nitrate, assisted by reducing bacteria in the traditional form of the process. The saltpeter, which is the natural form of potassium nitrate, is reduced by the bacteria, first into nitrite, and then into nitrous oxide, which combines with the red pigment of myoglobin.

Measuring 0.03% (200 ppm) is difficult to measure. It is practically resolved by the use of pre-blended cures. The trade offers Cure I, which contains 6.5% of active nitrite mixed with salt; or Cure II with a blend of nitrite and nitrate, Saltpeter is not allowed by USDA but food grade potassium nitrate can be found and used the same way.

The nitrite, resulting from the reduction of the nitrate, acts as a strong bacteriostatic; when it is further reduced to nitrous oxide it binds to myoglobin to form the characteristic bright red color of cured meats; then it evaporates. This chemical transformation multiplies the preserving effects of the salt. This process is the result of a natural biological action, which takes time: a day or two in comminuted sausages, a week or more, depending on the size, in whole muscles. During that time the bacterial activity also creates aromas and flavors, which are unique to the cured meats. The meat texture and taste are modified and the mouth-feel of the products changes.

Curing is visible; after one or two days, the color changes to red from grey while at the same time the proteins start binding.

Curing is perceptible to the touch; meat or sausage become firmer. In French there is the expression "Le saucisson prend la main", (The sausages takes the hand), reflecting the change from pasty to rubbery.

The full penetration of the salt and the chemistry of the nitrate reduction, in particular the nitrite phase; eliminates or reduces the undesirable germs to an innocuous state. This is a very important part of the function of preserving the meat. It is supplemented by the acidification and the dehydration, after fermenting during the aging of salami and prosciutto; or, by smoking and cooking for other sausages and hams.

The traditional method, requiring plenty of time is also a warranty that the residual nitrate and nitrite, be negligible, when the product is ready to eat.

The curing salts are consumed during the natural process, and practically disappear from the product.

Modern science, penetrating the mystery of the cure and discovering the specific role of the nitrite, has allowed for the new technology of curing directly with nitrite; it doesn't require the activity of the bacteria; it is immediate, but either doesn't develop flavor and aroma.

The modern, fast-curing technique, via brine injection, is an invention of the mid 20th century.

When initially applied by the industry to bacon, in order to reduce the production time from more than a week to 48 hours, the quantity of nitrite used was not regulated. It led to abuse in order to get a quick deep red color to the bacon. Nitrite residual was high. When crisped at high temperature, that nitrite formed nitrosamine, which is considered a carcinogen.

When this was revealed, after a major media dramatization, the USDA established standards to control safe residual. Today, the scare is still used by marketers to claim "no nitrate or no nitrite" on some products; even if the same are cured with the nitrate occurring naturally in vegetable juice.

No nitrate-cooked sausages and hams are pale and insipid, but some play with the regulations, using the dehydrated juice of celery, which contains a high level of natural nitrate as a curing agent. It qualifies as flavoring for the label, which doesn't mention nitrate as an ingredient.

FERMENTING

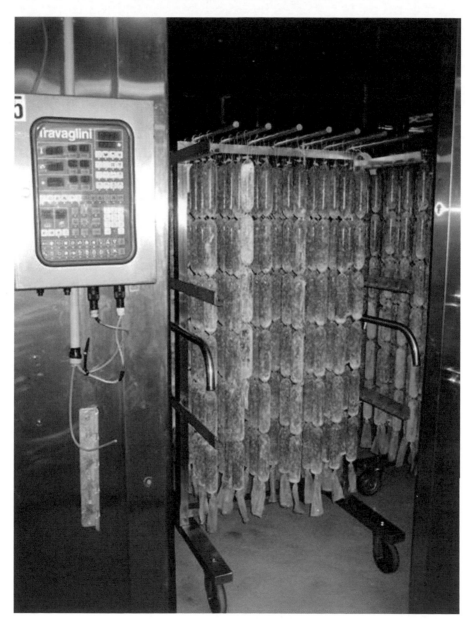

Salami after fermenting.

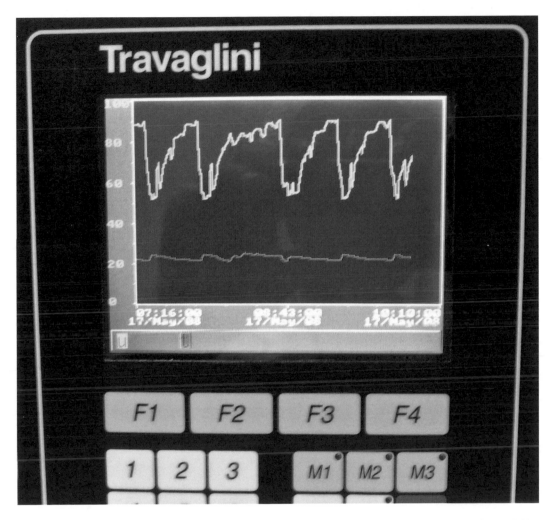

Environment control in a computerized room, white curve is relative humidity, red curve is temperature.

Here we enter a realm close to my heart - I like complexities and this is where we get close to life. This is where mind, heart and soul are needed to master the process with the right skills, with a full awareness to handle meats, fats, ingredients, casings, to set the tempo and modulate the right timing in the right environment to create the conditions, in which the bacteria and yeasts will perfect this work of art.

*Physics, biochemistry, microbiology will describe, in their many specialized departments, the complexities and the minutiae of every aspect in detail, every single note of the symphony, **but, it is for the player to deliver the harmony.***

Mastering fermentation is what makes a great vintner, a great baker, a great cheese-maker; likewise the great "salumiere" or "charcutier"… "sausage maker", does not partake in this aspect of the craft.

To help you understand this complex world, I added at the end of this book two documents prepared by Chr. Hansen, the company that dominates the production of starter cultures. First, you will get insight on the possibilities, the availability of different types of microorganism and how you can put them to work. Second, you will also see the many possible reasons to err and their remedy.

Here, it may be important to remember that before the development of modern hygiene and sanitizing, which imposes the use of starter cultures composed of a few selected microbes, fermenting relied on the balance of a more complex flora defining the "terroir" or the characteristics of each production place and people.

Now is the time to ponder why, in America, controlling the PH reduction from the fermentation, is the CCP (critical control point) for salami, and, secondarily, the Aw value or water/protein ratio, while in the CEE, the CCP is the level of the nitrate-nitrite and the shrinkage (25 % for small "salametti" and "cacciatori" and 30 % for large salami?

Is it because our system is based on the mass production of very acidic products sold very rapidly, while the Europeans take the time to slowly age much milder, better quality products?

Muscles contain a form of sugar (glycogen) that will ferment naturally, like grape juice, flour and other forms of carbohydrates with the help of microorganisms.

Tradition tells that Noah received the secret of making wine. I suspect that he was also making bread and salami, as the Italian continue to claim "salame, pane e vino" (salami, bread and wine… the secret of happy harmony).

Every meat paste contains some glycogen and a few germs, screened by the presence of salt, it is prone to ferment in some ways, unless the process is interrupted by another technique, like smoking and cooking.

Before the development of sanitation as we know it, old sausage kitchens or salami and prosciutto plants had a complex, in house-flora of meat germs occupying the ground, resisting intruders and delivering the typical taste and flavor of that specific producer. It was notorious that creating a new "salumificio" was a risky and lengthy proposition to establish a stable and safe flora in a new location.

Fermenting salami is more an art than a technique. The actual work is done by different types of bacteria also working in association with molds and yeasts. The bacterial life is sustained by sugar in some form, which they convert mostly to lactic acid. (Acetic acid and other compounds can also be produced, affecting the flavor profile). The acidification coagulates the myosin, initially solubilized by the salt, forming a gel and setting the paste. The soft ground meats become a solid, sliceable sausage.

The acidification also frees the water, which was bound to the protein and the salami can then progressively dry. It will quickly loose about 10% of its weight within the fermenting phase in 5-7 days, then, more slowly until ready after shrinkage of 30 to 35%.

The acidification of the meats at about PH6 is very mellow; only very slim products like "fuet", which stabilizes mostly from drying, can be at that level. The trade-off is very rich flavor. Most "salumi" of southern Europe have values of PH 5.3-5.6, like the best "felino", "sopressata" "saucisson secs" or "chorizo". A much stronger acidification, with values down to PH 4.2, is found in summer sausages, smoked German "Dauerwurst" and "Cervelat" or Danish salami.

Most American mainstream Genoa and other salami are produced in the lower range. Limited acidification leaves room for the formation of softer textures and richer aromas, while strong acidification yields a very tangy taste and firmness, accelerating greatly the processing time.

Most importantly, mellow acidification with the proper germs fighting competition of undesirable germs and sufficient time, results in some hydrolyzing of proteins and fats, thus developing welcomed natural aromas and flavor.

Fermenting, which results is acidification, setting and development of taste and flavors, is controlled by:

- The quality of the ingredients.

- The proper structure of the paste.

- The type and quality of the casing.

- The quantity and type of sugars, which can also come from sweet wine, spices or other ingredients.

- Inoculating the right type of bacterial ferments to develop acids and flavors

- The ideal environment, conditioning temperature, humidity and ventilation.

- The proper sequencing and timing.

Today, the use of specific starter cultures of beneficial microbes offers a simple solution to what were ancient problems. The type of starters varies, depending on the desired result, level of acidification, type of aroma and flavor.

Here again, the economic temptation will push for a heavy and fast acidification, in order to gain the quick setting of lesser quality salami and dry sausages e.g. summer sausage.

Instead the aim for quality will require a mellow and slower fermentation, to yield superior aroma, texture and flavor. It will also require more time for aging and add to the shrinkage.

We are lucky, today, to be able to choose amongst many types of ferments to achieve the desired result. But we can only control the activity of the ferments indirectly, initially, composing the paste, by the type of paste and ingredients; the added sugars are critically important to determine the desired level and speed of acidification and then during fermentation, by the handling and control of temperature, relative humidity, ventilation and time.

The best results depend on curing and fermenting at the lowest temperature. High humidity is necessary, initially to facilitate the heat transfer and to avoid "crusting" while the PH is still high (water is still bound to the proteins).

When the PH drops it is necessary to dehydrate the product as fast as possible, respecting the limit of what the salami can release without crusting.

This is the critical time when the hand of the **"salumiere" has to feel the salami and verify that it stays "happily" humid, not wet, nor dry,** while progressively reducing the temperature, trending to the aging environment.

Three interlocking phases:

- Cure and coagulate via acidification by bacterial life;
- Remove the free water to stop fermentation and stabilize the product;
- Grow outside molds and yeast, start the enzymatic maturing.

In the "salumiere" tradition, fermenting calls for the initial dripping ("sgocciolamento"), lasting a couple of days when the bacterial activity develops, with high humidity to facilitate the warming up of the salami toward 18° C with the room at 22° C. In this country we tend to maintain high humidity until the PH has dropped to the critical (USDA required) PH 5.2. Italians maintain the high humidity only for 8 hours to warm up the salami and start the fermentation. They start to extract briefly the humidity ("asciugamento") in the room, with a quick change of air or with the condensation on the coil. Then, they let the salami rest and "sweat" its humidity in the room back to high humidity and keep repeating the cycle. The advantage is a better control of the bacterial activity with a faster water reduction and the reduction of mold and yeast growth.

---

*Here I need to insist. Proper fermenting is key to success, but do not get fixated there; "bugs" will work for a while anyway, as long as there is enough water and sugar for them. **Drying as fast as the salami will allow,** is as important, not only for quality, cleanness and mildness, but also for your economic performance. (Huge difference if your salami is ready in 3 rather than 6 weeks). Do not keep the salami in warm high humidity too long; help it shed its excess water soon after warm-up; do it without stressing and crusting it. This is where you will need your finest senses and feeling, unless you have, and even if you do, a fine programmed fermenting room.*

Dehydrating and resulting salt concentration stops the fermenting. Mastering the strength of the acidification controls the degree of tanginess.

The following phase, during which molds and yeast starts to grow on the casing, develops the aroma. It takes about a week of intensive care; during this time the salami shrinks by about 12%. Mold and yeasts have established themselves on the casing and the room smells very good. The salami is ready to transit to the aging process.

When I smell the salami at this stage and feel it cool, silky in my hand, I can't refrain to take out my knife and cut a wheel. It is a double pleasure; first because at this stage the salami is like a fresh mozzarella, mild, sweet, aromatic and very satisfying; second because it is a forbidden pleasure since here USDA doesn't allow the consumption unless the water/protein ratio reaches 1.9. It is a sweet memory of many delicious treats in the Old World where these restrictions don't apply.

The transition from dripping to drying to aging is a delicate affair to manage. The goal is to keep the salami "happy". It means avoiding stress and just evacuating whatever water it releases in the air of the room. Powerful coils can quickly capture the excess water; let the salami rest without the pull of ventilation and let it do its own thing quietly.

To determine how to operate, it is important to develop the feeling from the hand and fingers to sense how the salami is doing?

- **moist**; then, it is time to evacuate the humidity of the air. If it feels
- **dry** turn off the ventilation and let the salami rest until it regains it's just
- **humid** feeling.

The ancient job of the opening and closing of the windows, is replaced today by the adjusting of set points and time of computer controls.

FERMENTING, DRYING AND AGING

First, let the meats rest for a while, either stuffed in casing or bound and ready.

Start raising the temperature to about 70° F, let the humidity rise to saturation, until the product core reaches 65°F. Depending on the size, this will take from 6 to 12 hours.

This is the initial "Dripping" phase.

Then, change the air and start drying, with cycles of short drying of the room air, down to 60-65%, then letting the salami rest (that is very important), while the RH rises back up to 90%. Repeat the cycle, the rest time will last longer as the humidity within salami drops.

Progressively reduce the air temperature, (typically 4 ° F each day), to reach the aging phase at 50-55° F and reduce the RH set points to between 75% and 85%.

The time will depend also from the load in the drying room and the size, type of casing of the products.

The "setting" of the cured paste, is caused by the acidity; it is controlled by the type of culture, the quantity of sugar, the temperature in the paste (ideally below 65° F), and the free water available.

Here we recommend a cool and fast process, which will limit the acidity and resulting tanginess. The goal is to maximize instead the aroma and flavor.

Remember also that rapidly reducing the water activity, is the preferred European method of preserving meats safely.

Hand and fingers are the instruments of choice to guide the process, to assess the changes during curing and fermenting until the salami sets. Finger gliding on the casing can determine if it is wet, needing air, or dry needing to rest. The goal is to keep the casing surface just humid and the paste underneath flexible.

The smell of the salami fermenting, drying and molding will be a telling way to assess and manage the process.

Molds will grow under these conditions. Molds are part of the process and are good for the ripening of the salami; in this respect, mostly all kind of molds are beneficial, actually, variety will enhance the flavor.

Inseminate with a dip of white selected molds if the cosmetic look is an issue.

After a week to 10 days, the salami will age more gently, mature and finish drying at 75-80 % and 55° F.

Here are two examples of the way Italians control the fermenting process.

T = temperature ° C
U = relative humidity %
ore = hours
fase = phase

PROGRAM 1 small caliber products

Cooling:	T.min. 04	T. max. 06	U.min. 90	U.max. 95	ore 8:00
1) fase Dripping:	T.min. 21	T. max 23			ore 8:00
2) fase Drying :	T.min. 19	T. max. 21	U.min. 62	U.max. 77	ore 24:00
3) fase Drying	T.min. 17	T. max. 19	U.min. 66	U.max. 76	ore 24.00
4) fase Drying	T.min. 15	T. max. 17	U.min. 70	U.max. 77	ore 24:00
5) fase Drying	T.min. 14	T. max. 16	U.min. 73	U.max. 78	ore 24:00
6) fase Drying	T.min. 13	T. max. 15	U.min. 75	U.max. 80	ore 24:00
7) fase Aging	T.min. 12	T. max. 14	U.min. 77	U.max. 82	Infinite

PROGRAM 2 Bigger caliber products

Cooling	T.min. 04	T. max. 06	U.min. 90	U.max. 95	ore 8.00
1) fase Dripping:	T.min. 22	T. max 24			ore 8.00
2) fase Drying:	T.min. 20	T. max. 22	U.min. 60	U.max. 75	ore 24:00
3) fase Drying	T.min. 18	T. max. 20	U.min. 63	U.max. 75	ore 24:00
4) fase Drying	T.min. 17	T. max. 19	U.min. 67	U.max. 77	ore 24:00

5) fase Drying   T.min. 15   T. max. 17   U.min. 70   U.max. 78   ore 24:00

6) fase Drying   T.min. 14   T. max. 16   U.min. 72   U.max. 80   ore 24:00

7) fase Aging   T.min. 13   T. max. 15   U.min. 75   U.max. 80   Infinite

Typical recording of a dripping and drying initial phase

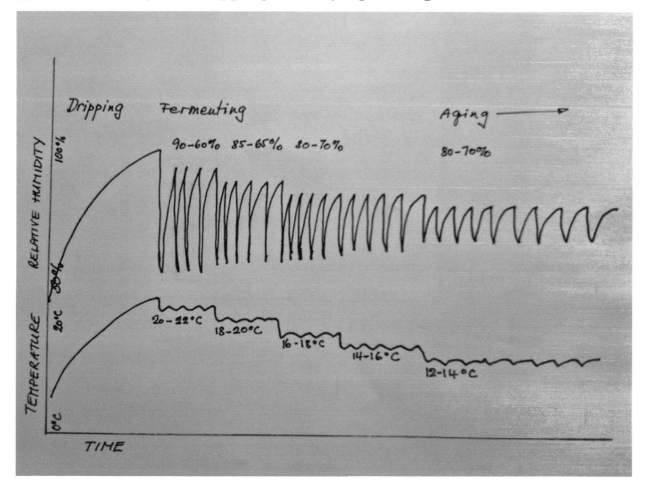

Note that the fermentation, which is commonly recommended in this country for a period of 48 H to 72 H, in high humidity, (point at which USDA requires the PH drop to 5.3) in Italy is handled differently, with the system extracting the excess humidity as

soon as the salami has been warmed up. The reason is to obtain a milder product and to limit the bacterial growth more quickly.

The salami evaporates its humidity in the room, where a cold evaporating coil can condensates it, without freezing the water to let it drain out.

Two set points control the system "Umax" triggers the drying, which is stopped at "Umin" (U, for Humidity in Italian).

Two temperature set points determine the "Tmax" and "Tmin", between which the room temperature operates. A heating coil is triggered if drying has not yet reached "Umin" and "Tmin" is reached (The drying cools the air).

As the programs above indicate, the set points vary during a complete phase from Dripping, Drying to Aging.
The general pattern has to be adjusted by frequent controls to take in account the type of product, casing and external influences.

The paramount goal is to keep the salami "happy", not wet, just humid and avoid the damaging crusting or case hardening.

Of course as in the case presented above, the art is to feel the salami state and translate it in the proper setting of the temperature, high and low point of the relative humidity to keep the product "happy".
The discussion should also consider the frequency and speed of air movement in the room, which are important factors in transferring the water from the surface of the salami to the air and to the condensing coil.
The system cannot go faster than the salami's ability to bring the water to the surface. Here too, balance and harmony are the condition of "happiness".

SMOKING

The most primitive tribes of hunters and fishermen know how to use smoke.

Smoking is originally a way to preserve perishable meats, fish or cheese. The components of the smoke are bactericides.

The many components of the smoke are to a degree soluble; they will penetrate the casing of the meat or sausage, adding a strong and characteristic smell and aroma to the product.

Smoking foods is a Nordic tradition in Europe, originating in the forests of the north; instead, the mediterranean peoples have a way of molding as a consequence of preserving the "salumi" in the cool and humid cellar, after fermentation in the warm kitchen.

Interestingly, the fermentation was often done, in the past, in rooms where the warmth required was produced by the burning of charcoals, also generating a little smoke, giving a light and delicious smoky touch to the ancient "salumi".

Hickory wood is in America, like the beech wood in Europe; the main source of smoke. Resinous fir is used in the Black forest. Specialties can be smoked with apple wood or juniper. Alder, cottonwood and possibly many other species are also used as regional specialties.

Some spike the smoke with the addition of aromatic herbs and spices.

The smoke is generated from sawdust, chips or logs. The wood is usually dry, but sometimes soaked in water to reduce the burning temperature, this plays an important role for the composition of the smoke and the resulting flavor.

Generating the smoke and applying it to the meat is still done in many different ways, though, the programmed smoke oven is nowadays the basic instrument.

Today, the purpose of smoking is more for flavoring and visual appearance than rather preservation. What determine the quality of the color and flavor is:

- The choice of the wood type.
- The conditioning of the wood, wet or dry.
- The generation temperature and relative humidity.
- The temperature and skin condition of the product in the oven.

Depending on the type of wood, the temperature and humidity, all kinds of active chemicals are released, some beneficial and pleasant, some harsh and tarry and are to be avoided.

It is possible to find smoke extract, which can be applied as spray on the surface of meats or incorporated in the injection brine. None reach the quality of the real good process.

Hot smoking is done for a limited time, in the order of one hour prior to the final cooking of sausages, when the casing is dry and able to absorb the smoke, at a cooking temperature.

Cold smoking is used for meats destined to be dry aged, it requires a much longer time at much lower temperatures, which have to stay below the fat melting point.

In between, bacon is often hot smoked without reaching full cooking; it is the best way to finish dry-cured bellies for an aromatic and tasty bacon, dry enough to keep well and crisps readily without the first boiling out of the injected kind.

The generation of the smoke is done in many different ways, from the fire box of a Texan BBQ outfit, to the hot plate of a smoke generator associated with a programmable oven or the simple burning of wet sawdust at the bottom of a cabinet. In Italy, a big steel pan, loaded with burning charcoals was slid on the floor under the salamis, hanging off the ceiling to ferment and initiate the drying, which was adjusted by the proper opening of the room window. In Schleswig-Holstein, home of the famous "Katenschinken", the hams hang under the thatched roof of a barn (the "Katen") and age in a very light and cold smoke for months. In the Jura mountains, the farms of Morteau are built around a central vast smoke room, called "tué", in which "jambons" et "saucissons" are immersed in cold fir wood smoke.

Cold smoke is applied briefly and repeatedly over a longer period. It can be applied before or during fermentation, even later after an initial drying and aging.

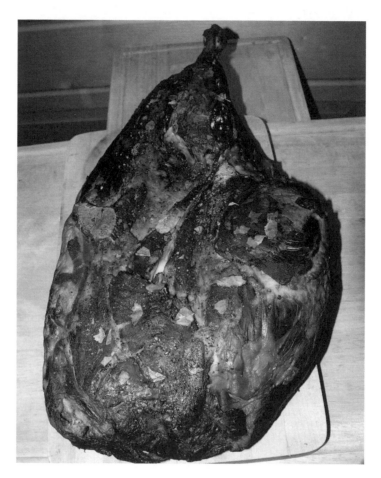

Speck Tirolese.

COOKING

The smoky exposure to the open fire or the grilling over hot coals are still good options today. The heat acts in three ways: primarily coagulating proteins; eliminating germs but also modifying the texture of the meat, the critical temperature for this effect is in the order of 150° F.

Cooking, even when done in saturated humidity or water, always extracts some water from the meat; this drying is at least 10% of the weight of the meat. It is a function of the temperature and the time. It can be a desirable effect to augment taste, nutrition and stability, or can be compensated, if the meat has been injected, at a minimum to balance the cooking loss or even to obtain a cooked weight superior to the green weight.

Baking is the method used to cook "mortadella" and some hams. During warming up in non-saturated air, (damper open), the cold meat of large pieces will stay long enough at fermenting temperature and gain during this stage definite flavor characteristics. The further cooking to reach the pasteurization temperature is slower than water cooking. The shrinkage, caused by this mode, is beneficial. It increases the density and texture, and reduces the water activity in the product. It is made more stable, has a longer shelf life and better taste.

Roasting will add specific changes to the meats, resulting in increased appeal, better ,appearance, smell, taste and texture. At the higher reaches of temperature, past the boiling point, water is actively extracted, sugars caramelize, the protein and fat are modified and generating new flavors. Roasting doesn't need to penetrate the core of whole muscles; they are naturally sterile, unless they have been injected. Made thusly a "rare" and juicy roast beef is safe. Instead in the case of sausages or injected meats the core has to be pasteurized. If done under the roasting temperature large pieces will be over cooked externally when critical temperature is reached and shrinkage will be excessive. Convection ovens or "combi-ovens" with programmable temperature and ideal humidity are able to cook slowly at minimal temperature to reach pasteurization without significant shrinkage and outside crusting.

The injected industrial roast beef, pastrami, corned beef and all the ham and poultry luncheon meats are steam cooked. In order to label them as roast, surface flaming or coloring with blood are used to create the illusion of actual roasting.

Barbecueing in the southern or Texan way submits the meats to indirect fire and smoke for a time long enough to actually **braise** the meats. This is the point where the collagen, bundling the muscle fibers, converts in the presence of steam to gelatin. This changes the meat texture, fibers become loose and tender, tough sinews become juicy and gelatinous.

The ultimate **braising**, completely loosening the muscle fibers yields the meat of the luau or in Hawaii, or in Mexico, the "carnitas".

Frying is not a common way of processing meats, but rendering leaf fat for lard actually fries the cracklings. Similarly, the Mexican "chicharones" are skins fried in their fat after tenderizing by boiling.

The art of cooking belongs to the chef, but the sausage maker needs to share the awareness of the many techniques if only to create the product that will best be steamed, boiled, baked or grilled.

MOLDING

Crespone blooming.

Wild molds and yeasts have an affinity for meats and sausage casings; they can develop and colonize the whole surface if the environment is to their liking. Excessively wet surface support the growth of bacteria, which will form slime. Molds like a humid but not wet environment. Salami or dry-cured meats, which are going through a high humidity dripping phase, must rapidly be dried to avoid the possibility of forming slime and transit to the humid stage to allow the growth of the mold.

Molds, often accompanied by yeasts, are beneficial; they do not produce toxin when growing on proteins. They form a buffer layer between the meat, slowly drying and the air circulating around. They add their own enzymes into the meats; they improve texture and create desired flavor during aging.

Originally occurring in the cool and moist environment of the "cantina" where wine, cheeses, roots, cured meats and salami were kept, or nowadays in the dedicated aging room, they were occasional natural molds brought in by the environment.

As in the curing room, bacteria form a specific flora in the aging room; molds and yeasts would establish themselves as a specific environment, another factor of the flavor and aroma of the local products.

Wild molds that grow on proteins are mostly **penicilia**, which occur in different shapes and color. American consumers are afraid of mold and, if present, will only tolerate white mold as they have learned lately to accept on Brie cheese.

A class of "foodies" has reached the point where they reject salami which is not molded. It happens, I guess, when these Americans travel to Europe and attend shows and visit shops there. <I am glad to see this happening in the East though it was never a problem in northern California home of the "Italian dry salame" of San Francisco, always molded >. Still I wonder when I see a "Genoa" produced in the East, stuffed in a white, washed casing and usually shipped vacuum packaged.

The penicillia are, in nature, wood decaying molds. Their ability to digest cellulose can have a destructive effect on fibrous casings.

I have seen salami, kept too humid, with the casing disappearing and the mold transferring directly to the meat.

In Italy, I have tasted rustic salami made at the farm, covered with black mold. They were fantastic, incredibly tasty. Here they would have been thrown away.

Today, molds and possibly yeasts are inoculated from starter cultures, selected for their white, cosmetic coverage. We gain in look and acceptance, but we loose bouquet and aroma.

Molds also act as a natural anti-oxidant and protect the salami from rancidity.

Inoculating is done after the stuffing by immersion or spraying of water containing the spores of the molds and yeast, the process is facilitated by the addition of a gelling agent, to the water to help the adherence of the spores to the casings.

Aging Prosciutti.

AGING

Enzymes are present in the meat itself and come from the other participants in the process - bacteria, molds, yeasts, natural casings, and even from some ingredients. Over time, during the aging of the cured meats and salami, enzymes allow for the slow modification of the proteins and fats. The enzymatic chemistry tends to fracture the long molecules of the proteins and the fats (it is called hydrolyzing). The resulting compounds are aromatic.

I think of the soybean fermenting in a similar way, becoming the tasty soy sauce.

The hydrolyzing occurring over time is also perceptible as a change of color and as the softer texture due to a fragmentation of the muscle and membrane proteins. The hydrolyzing of the fat is noticeable when small pearls of oil exude from the fresh cut salami, solid fat has become, in part, free fatty acids contributing to the flavor.

"Il salame fa la perla". So say the Italians, when they cut a mature salami and see droplets of oil coming out. It is a sure sign of maturity.

Each product has its own way of aging; some like the "saucisson" will benefit from a couple of weeks. Salami, depending on their size and the type of texture will be ready in a few weeks or a few months. "Coppa" a few months; "prosciutto" and "culatello" will require at least a whole year and often more.

To manage aging, you will need all of your acute senses and a bit of intuition. There is no standard since aging depends on every possible factor - to begin with, the meat itself, the processing, every single ingredient, then the externals, casing, molds yeasts and finally the conditions of the environment they all play a role.

It takes cutting and tasting, or as with prosciutto the long thin and pointed bone of the horse leg to poke into the ham alongside the femur to capture the aroma building and decide when to ship.

Massimo Spigaroli, who ages "culatelli, in the cellar of the castle of Antica Corte Pallavicina on the banks of the Po river, near Parma, made me taste the "culatello" at one, two and three years. The meat of a three-years old "culatello", literally, was melting in my mouth and filling my nose with subtle and delicious aroma.
That is the kind of experience you want to share someday.

Aging never stops adding refinement to a product, but, it can get overwhelmed, when excessive de-hydrating, or oxidation sets rancidity in the fat. This progressive decay of aged meat products progresses from the periphery and can be trimmed away to regain a bright and blooming core.

Italian old-timers will tell you how to salvage a salami or an overly dry "salumi": trim it clean, wrap it in a towel soaked in wine, enclose it in a plastic foil or in a bag and let it rest in you fridge for a few days… you will be pleasantly surprised by the result.

Aging care of the whole muscles

Closely follow the dry cured whole muscles, check them regularly while they dry and age. The duration will be determined by their condition. Molds, possibly slime, cracks due to excessive drying, release of oil due to hydrolyzing, beginning of rancidity are limiting factors you have to watch for.

Sound, high-quality pork will allow for longer aging and better results.

Heavy prosciutto, "culatello" are likely to keep about a year, but can be held for more than two years.

"Coppa" and "pancetta" keep about 3-6 months.

Salami in natural casing, if large enough (diameter above 100 mm, 4") can benefit up to 6-8 months of aging.

Temperature, ideally 8-10° C, along with very low air movement and RH, 85 % are very important factors affecting the duration of aging.

PACKAGING

The industry has habituated us to equate packaging to plastic. Impermeable films constitute a barrier behind which meats, quasi sterile or protected by stabilizer can keep for weeks, a necessity in the long distance and time required in modern distribution.

The consequence may be better hygiene, but also acidification and taste degradation, which guarantees a bland, if not stale, product when finally consumed. This applies to a lesser degree, for dry-aged, meat products, but is certainly the case with the high water luncheon meats, which are so popular in our supermarket delis.

These kinds of meat products should be consumed fresh to be enjoyed at the peak of their quality.

Compare the experience of being served hand-cut prosciutto or "mortadellla" at the counter with aromas wafting to your nose, with instead, using scissors to cut the plastic and trying to break loose sticky slices with greasy fingers!

Dry cured meats and salami have to be shipped before they reach their full maturity, while they still need to breathe, in order to reach the consumer at their peak. Shipping boxes with openings, maintained in a cool and slightly humid environment are best, but never leave them in the same cooler as citrus or onions!

"Salumi" can be wrapped in permeable butcher paper, for the trip home or the storage in the fridge. When they get dry, then it is time to switch to the plastic wrap or the convenient Zip-Lock. The same is true for the smoked sausages.

Cooked products wrapped in butcher paper should be consumed within days and kept refrigerated; vacuum packaged, they will certainly keep longer but the temptation will be to keep them too long, when they will loose the best of their flavor and turn sour; however they should still be bacteriologically safe.

Steaming or pan browning, depending on the kind of sausage or ham, can revive stale products, which are otherwise still sound.

Charcutier. Salumiere. Wurstmeister.

As we have seen all along this work, the building of peak quality and flavor is incompatible with long routes and extensive storage.

*Starting with meats and ingredients, which need to be fresh for processing, the same is true of the products themselves and calls, for the same reasons, for the "locavores" wisely recommended slogan **"eat close to home"**.*

COMPUTING AND CONTROL

https://skydrive.live.com/edit.aspx?cid=6FCAB7A516EEF0A2&resid=6FCAB7A516EE F0A2%21107&app=Excel

The Excel file is accessible to the public if you are registered in Microsoft SkyDrive. You can also ask me to send you a file at: mailto:franvec@gmail.com.

Controlling the economy of the process of breaking a whole pig and selling a variety of products and keeping control of the individual costs and different yields.

In this Excel spread sheet (Sheet 1), the whole process is documented; the formulas are set. Some information, in the red columns, have to be measured and entered. In the blue columns, values have to be entered in order to achieve the compounded target value (in darker red on top).

In this case the sheet deals with Pork sides without head, kidney and leaf lard.

With some experience in Excel, it is easy to adjust the matrix to the actual situation.

Sheet 2 and 3 gives the yield % of very different type of pork and of a head-on and offal yield.

7/4/09 BUTCHER HOG W/O HEAD, SALUMIERE 4/5 RIB, LONG HAM

	WHOLE	@ VALUE	VALUE	PRODUCTS	Ingred.	meat+In.	process	yield	cost	PROCESSED VALUE	Distr	sell	MARKET VALUE
Cost of meat	98.24%	$ 2.55	$ 2.20 100%		$ 0.35					$ 4.35 50.61%			$ 5.29 41.60%
shoulder	**36.09%**												
foot	1.57%	$ 0.20	$ 0.0031							0.00314			$ 0.00314
bone	2.55%	$ 0.20	$ 0.0051							0.00510			$ 0.00510
riblets	0.69%	$ 2.50	$ 0.0173							0.01725			$ 0.01725
coppa	5.98%	$ 3.50	$ 0.2093	coppa	$ 0.40	$ 0.02	$ 3.90	$ 2.50	70.00% $ 9.14	0.38272	$ 0.30	$ 12.00	$ 0.50232
flaps	2.75%	$ 3.00	$ 0.0825	salami	$ 0.50	$ 0.01	$ 3.50	$ 3.58	70.00% $ 10.12	0.19477	$ 0.25	$ 9.00	$ 0.17325
cushion	1.76%	$ 3.00	$ 0.0528	salami	$ 0.50	$ 0.01	$ 3.50	$ 2.00	70.00% $ 7.86	0.09680	$ 0.25	$ 9.00	$ 0.11088
Pork II	8.73%	$ 2.50	$ 0.2183	salami	$ 0.50	$ 0.04	$ 3.00	$ 2.00	70.00% $ 7.14	0.62357	$ 0.25	$ 8.00	$ 0.48888
bones	2.35%	$ 0.20	$ 0.0047							0.00470			$ 0.00470
skin	2.06%	$ 0.50	$ 0.0103							0.01030			$ 0.01030
50/50	2.45%	$ 1.50	$ 0.0368	sausage	$ 0.45	$ 0.02	$ 1.95	$ 1.00	90.00% $ 3.28	0.07228	$ 0.20	$ 5.00	$ 0.11025
butt fat	5.20%	$ 1.50	$ 0.0780	salami	$ 0.50	$ 0.02	$ 2.00	$ 2.00	70.00% $ 5.71	0.29714	$ 0.25	$ 8.00	$ 0.29120
long ham	**30.10%**												
foot	1.18%	$ 0.20	$ 0.0024							0.00236			$ 0.00236
inside peeled	4.41%	$ 3.50	$ 0.1544	ham	$ 0.25	$ 0.02	$ 3.75	$ 1.00	90.00% $ 5.28	0.20948	$ 0.25	$ 6.00	$ 0.23814
Pork II	1.08%	$ 2.50	$ 0.0270	salami	$ 0.50	$ 0.02	$ 3.00	$ 2.00	70.00% $ 7.14	0.07714	$ 0.25	$ 8.00	$ 0.06048
skin	1.47%	$ 0.50	$ 0.0074							0.00735			$ 0.00735
50/50	1.18%	$ 1.50	$ 0.0177	sausage	$ 0.45	$ 0.02	$ 1.95	$ 1.00	90.00% $ 3.28	0.03481	$ 0.20	$ 5.00	$ 0.05310
fat (traces of lean)	2.35%	$ 1.00	$ 0.0235	sausage	$ 0.35	$ 0.02	$ 1.35	$ 1.00	90.00% $ 2.61	0.06136	$ 0.20	$ 5.00	$ 0.10575
bones	2.84%	$ 0.20	$ 0.0057							0.00568			$ 0.00568
speck	15.59%	$ 3.00	$ 0.4677	speck	$ 0.40	$ 0.02	$ 3.40	$ 2.75	75.00% $ 8.20	0.95879	$ 0.30	$ 12.00	$ 1.40310
center	**32.05%**												
tender	1.18%	$ 5.00	$ 0.0590							0.05900			$ 0.05900
spareribs	2.84%	$ 3.00	$ 0.0852							0.08520			$ 0.08520
boneless loin	6.27%	$ 3.50	$ 0.2195	Roast	$ 0.15	$ 0.02	$ 3.65	$ 1.50	80.00% $ 6.44	0.32291	$ 0.25	$ 10.00	$ 0.50160
back ribs	0.59%	$ 4.00	$ 0.0236							0.02360			$ 0.02360
bones	1.96%	$ 0.20	$ 0.0039							0.00392			$ 0.00392
flank & blades	1.37%	$ 3.00	$ 0.0411	salami	$ 0.50	$ 0.02	$ 3.50	$ 2.00	70.00% $ 7.86	0.07535	$ 0.25	$ 9.00	$ 0.08631
skin	2.55%	$ 0.50	$ 0.0128							0.01275			$ 0.01275
pancetta	5.59%	$ 3.00	$ 0.1677	pancetta	$ 0.40	$ 0.02	$ 3.40	$ 2.25	80.00% $ 7.06	0.31584	$ 0.23	$ 9.00	$ 0.40248
backfat & belly straps	5.78%	$ 1.50	$ 0.0867	salami	$ 0.50	$ 0.02	$ 2.00	$ 2.00	70.00% $ 5.71	0.23120	$ 0.25	$ 8.00	$ 0.32368
50/50	2.16%	$ 1.50	$ 0.0324	sausage	$ 0.45	$ 0.02	$ 1.95	$ 1.00	90.00% $ 3.28	0.06372	$ 0.20	$ 5.00	$ 0.09720
Pork II	1.76%	$ 2.50	$ 0.0440	salami	$ 0.50	$ 0.02	$ 3.00	$ 2.00	70.00% $ 7.14	0.08800	$ 0.25	$ 8.00	$ 0.09856

Summary:

PORK I	5.88%
PORK II	11.57%
fat	10.98%
SALAMI	**28.43%**
50/50	5.79%
fat + trace	2.35%
SAUSAGE	**8.14%**

In Sheet 1 (best if you follow directly on your computer)

- On top, the original material cost, in this case whole pork.

- First column (B) the results of boning and trimming in per cents. Put in the actual yields.

- Second column (C), a possible value, as a "what if?" The factored percentile value, to match the actual cost. If you lower some you have to increase other.

- In third column (D), sums up the compounded value to match the cost of Pork.

- Fourth (F) A list of the products.

- Fifth (G), the specific ingredients cost per unit of fresh meat. Figure the actual cost per unit of fresh meat.

- Sixth (H), factors the Ingredients cost into the overall meat cost.

- Seventh (I), the combined cost of meat and ingredients.

- Eighth (J), figure your labor and overhead per unit of product.

- Ninth (K), control the actual processing yield to the finished product.

- Tenth (L), computes your cost per product.

- Eleventh (M), factors the individual products back into the compounded average cost of materials at the sales level.

- Twelve (N), add your sales and distribution costs.

- Thirteenth (O), Input the net selling price. (Deduct sampling, shrinkage, returns and spoils. Adjust value to the target average selling price in:

- Fourteenth (P), to compound the result of the (O) input.

If you can find an antique like my friend Mike Phillips did, you are sure to be the focus of all attention and get raving comments on your fine "salumi".

SLICING

Slicing is part of preparing the meat product. It is an important aspect of how the product is going to be perceived and enjoyed.

It demands a lot of attention and needs to anticipate the way the product will produce the best effect.

- Slice across the length of the muscle fibers.
- Thinly slice, just at the time of consumption in order to avoid venting of the aroma when preparing dry aged products like prosciutto.
- Thicker slice for tasty and mellow salami, when chewing into a smooth texture is part of the enjoyment.
- Slant slicing of large salami to enlarge the visual appeal of the slice.
- Julienne of spicy salami to top a salad.
- Shaved thin, curly slices of a very dry "Buendnerfleisch" or "pancetta piana".
- Shave "Lardo" over a hot grilled bread slice.
- But bite directly into a "Cacciatore", skin, mold and all. If you don't dare, cut a thick chunk for a mouthful.

TASTING

All our senses need to be attending the celebration of a perfected product. Experience and attention is required to perceive directly every aspect and to avoid the trap of habits or mediated images and concepts imposed externally.

- First, the look.
- Then, the smell.
- Test with your fingers, feel the texture, the cohesion of the slice.
- On the tongue, first sense the salt, the tang, the sweet, the bitter, linger up to the "umami" and *"je ne sais quoi?"*
- In the mouth, feel the bite, the texture of lean and fat, chunky, smooth, sleek or rough.
- Back to the nose, via the palate, sense the aroma, subtle flavor, fines nuances.
- After swallowing, follow the finish. Then feel, eventually the spicy heat.
- Pay attention to the aftertaste, it reveals a lot about the substance.
- Get the feeling of the throat, clean, smooth and happy or bitter and harsh.

"Il buon salame lascia la bocca pulita", (the good salami leaves the mouth clean). Is your tummy happy? …Stomach dialing the brain, asking for more, is the best way to experience and know true quality.

CLEANING

Under today's regulations, there is not a lot left to your judgment, when it comes to sanitation procedures.

It used to be part of keeping the right balance of natural flora and contains the bacterial, insect, molds and yeast activity to an efficient level. The principle was to keep things clean, dry and well aerated. Wood was part of the system as a slight bacteriostatic, easy to clean and maintain. On the floor sawdust was spread instead of water.

Today's systems meant to destroy all germs, creates the risk of high moisture in hidden cracks and crevasses, where the "nasties" can hold ground. The recommended plastic and steel surfaces get dings and scratches where they can hide.

There again, your open senses, in particular smell, will alert you when things go out of control.

Now that you have penetrated the spirit and are anxious to do, let me make some suggestions. These recipes are "basic", they cover about every type of what is traditionally done with pork. Use them as a frame, as a guide, for you to determine what you want to achieve.

We consider numbers as concrete; in fact, they represent variable qualities since no product, ingredient, spice and environment are equal and constant. It is time to apply your finesse and take charge.

Get your hands dirty, practice, experience, learn and share.

SALUMI, CHARCUTERIE, EMBUTIDOS, WURST

Or how to use the whole pork

We propose 40 typical pork products to use the whole of the pork from the different European cultures (Italian, French, Spanish, German, Swiss). Each one is different, not only by the ingredients involved, but mostly by using different techniques or gradations within a set processing.

We can find each product in the world in many local variations under different names corresponding to the specific tastes, traditions, circumstances and usages of the place.

Full knowledge of the materials, ingredients and clear understanding and handling of the technical steps allow for infinite variations, allow for the creativity of the Master.

MEAT SPECIFICATION

The quality of products depends to a large part from the components in the meat:

- Red muscle proteins.
- White collagen and elastin membranes and sinews.
- Fat, hard or soft, containing more or less membranes.

Noble products are made with cleaned red muscle (Pork I) and hard fat.

Increase in membrane (Pork II) adds a gelatinous component.

Soft fat has to be emulsified to stay incorporated or will render away.

The following trimming selections allow for the formulation of products according to specific purposes.

Pork yields other parts beyond meat and fat, like blood and organs all of them destined to particular products.

Pork I de-sinewed 95% lean.

Pork II with membranes and sinews 90% lean.

Pork Belly lean 40/60% fat.

Pork 70/30 commodity standard trim.

Pork 50/50.

Jowl or Butt Fat 20/80% very hard fat.

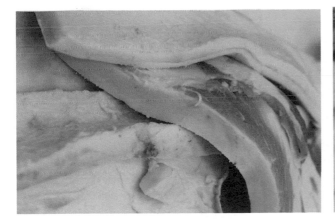

Back Fat 10/90% hard fat.

Mouilles soft fat.

Leaf lard.

Tail, trotters.

Head: Cheek, tongue, ear, snout, brain.

Organs: Liver, heart, spleen, kidneys, lungs.

Intestines: Small and large, tripe, caul fat.

Blood.

Bones.

SKINS

In Europe, mostly in the nordic tradition, skins are incorporated in most emulsified sausages..

The advantage is to add juiciness since the collagen of the skin will turn into gelatin during cooking.

The **"Schwartenblok"** (skin block) is used as a pre-processed component in the formulation at a rate of 10 to 20%. The block is pre cut and ground or chopped with all the other meats and ingredients.

There are two ways of preparing the skins, they must be completely lean; all fat must be trimmed. This is difficult to achieve by hand but easily done by the de-rinding machines.

- Pre-cooked with salt (1%) ground then blended with just enough broth to reduce it to a smooth gel and let set in an open container.
- Raw, demanding a progressive reduction of particle size, through successive grinding with plates of diminishing size, since skins are extremely hard to break. When reduced to a 1 or 1.5 mm, they can be blended at high speed in the chopper with addition of ice, until a gelling slurry is formed and let set as a block of convenient size in an ad hoc container.

Consuming the skin of the pork, instead of tanning it, is established by tradition. It always has been the natural packaging for the ham and bacon. It is also because of the tight adherence of the best fat that it is so difficult to remove the skin.

The Italian "salumiere" sorts the best meats for his salami and works the skin in the "cotechino". He stuffs a premium "zampone" in the front leg skin, even in stitched skin "capello di prete".

The "charcutier Lyonnais" sorts the best for his "saucisse de Lyon" ("saucisson") and the skins for the "sabaudet" (probably for the ancient name of Savoy "Sabaudia"). In Geneva the "longeole" is a similar sausage, flavored with fennel seeds, containing a third of ground skin, which requires simmering for two or three hours to bring about its perfect juiciness and sticky texture.

BARDIERE (BACK FAT SHEET)

Thin sheets of fat are used to garnish or cover "pâtés". The butchers of Paris wrap every "rosbif" to protect it and enrich the gravy.

It is a cumbersome job to slice 3 mm (1/8") from a flattened piece of back fat. The top layer anyway tends to be broken and too soft.

A more efficient way is to use the deli slicer. After removing the carriage, adjust the spacer at the desired thickness. Place the back fat on the spacer, press down while pulling (like gliding) the back fat against the blade, use a slot in the skin, to insert a hook for traction and keep your fingers off the blade.

Keep repeating until the blade reaches the skin. The last "bardières", close to the skin will be the best.

INGREDIENTS

This is a quick review of what we discussed at length before.
Salt: Preferably unrefined salts like sea or rock salt. Natural salts contain in small quantity all kinds of other minerals, which play an important role in the harmony and balance of the complex salting, curing and fermenting process. It translates into rounder and more balanced flavor.

The size of the salt crystal is important in dry-curing, to control the speed and quantity of it absorbing into the meat

Cure: The critically active ingredient is the **nitrite,** which can derive, via the microbial reduction from **nitrate,** which also flavors the meat. It is usually available as cure I, which contains only nitrite; or cure II with nitrite and some nitrate.

The ancient curing salt is **saltpeter** or potassium nitrate.

The use of nitrate only requires the activity of the fermenting bacteria to be effective.

The recipes indicate the percent of salt to be applied to the meat block and the mention eventually: **cure**. *It is left to your judgment to ad the proper cure, depending on your circumstances. The quantities involved are so small that they do not significantly affect the total salt, which anyway, you will adjust to your taste.*

Sugars: As sweetener and fermenting support. Sugars are carb chains of different length; the short chain dextrose or fructose ferment faster than longer sucrose or even longer maltose; the length of the carb chain increases further in ingredients like maltodextrin, which does not ferment and act as a binder or extender, all the way to the starches.

Spices: Pepper, garlic and onions are the basic. The variety is vast and the possibilities unlimited, though their usage has to be limited to support and enhance the meat, not to overwhelm or hide it.

It is tempting to use cheaper less quality meat and faster process covered up with strong spicing. This leads to all these vulgar, hard to digest sausages and hot dogs, which cause reflux and burping in our rebelling stomach.

Instead the art consists of orchestrating the quality of the meat, the fineness of the process, the play of time and balance of the natural agents to express with the complement of light spicing, the genuine flavor and aroma of the product.

Wine: Preferably sweet and aromatic; sometime spirits are used for their flavor.
Starter Cultures: There are many types of beneficial organisms. It includes the ferments active inside the meat and also the mold and yeast for the casings.

It is important to research and test those that will best fit the recipe and the process. *Review the Chr. Hansen Bactoferm pamphlet in addenda.*

Casings: Prefer the naturals. They all enhance flavor and best protect the products.

The large intestines are thicker, protect the products better and impart flavor like the pork bungs and chitterlings ("crespone", "filzetta", "culare") or beef bungs; the small intestines are leaner and fit the smaller sausages or faster drying salami.

Collagen casing and films are the next best thing,

Fibrous (cellulose) is strong and convenient, but does not improve the products.

You can get a lot of detailed information on the site of my friends Mike and David Mayo of Oversea Casing <www.overseacasing.com>

Twine: Use only the hemp fiber; spool on a small hand size dowel and soak thoroughly before using.

DECIMAL SYSTEM AND PERCENTAGES

The decimal system can be used with a scale set on kilograms or pounds allowing the decimal fractions.

Recipes given in %, allow for accuracy and flexibility when preparing the meat and ingredients.

Using the metric system is the best practice, since it gives a clear relation, between kilogram and liter (mass and volume, one liter of water weighs one kilo) it is the practical way to avoid the lb./pint, oz./spoon confusion.

With my European education I always wonder why my US friends still struggle trying to untangle the limited way recipes are given here.

To me a recipe is only an abstract set representation of what I have to express, using actual meats, fat and other ingredients. The connection to the qualities, which I can sense, lead me to adjust and fine tune, sometime even introduce variations that the real situation induces. So, I left a space for your own notes on each page of recipes, to let you refine the formula in accordance with your circumstances.

By Salt and Cure I give a level of salting for the specific product the mode of curing is left to the preparer. I always prefer to use the potassium nitrate, the good old saltpeter in combination with an adequate starter culture, it may consume more time but the result is always tastier.

So, percentages eliminate the confusing and rigid use of pounds, pints, cups, spoons and their fractions; when it comes to grinding plate size it would be natural for me to give you a size in millimeters, 3.5, 5, 8 are the most commonly used, for me it is immediate and visual. I "see" the right plate, but you guys stick to your 3/16, 1/4 3/8, 5/8 and I nearly get a headache to figure which one it is.

America some day will have to go metric, so I will help in this direction and plates will go metric in these recipes.

THE TOOLS OF THE TRADE

What You'll Need:

- A well ventilated, refrigerated room
- Large sink, plenty of hot water, good drains.
- Fridge and freezer to hold and condition the meat
- Large cutting table.
- Sharp knives, a bone saw, steel and sharpening stone.

- Containers, sheet-pans or bins to hold the product.

- Scales; large and small with tare and decimal fractions for the pounds.

- Grinder with different plates—making sure that the plates and knives cut and not crush the meat; keep the pairs, each plate with it's own knife, always together.

- Bowl chopper or blender as food processor for emulsifying.

- Mixer (often called blender by butchers).

- Stuffer.

- Cooker, a big pot of water to set the sausage, render lard, make stock or cook the ham, or possibly a combi-oven.

- Fermenting room preferably sourced in Italy, with programmed processing.

- Trays, grates, hanging sticks and wagons.

- Oven for smoking, cooking, possibly fermenting and drying.

- Aging room, a good cellar or a cool attic.

- Thermometer, hygrometer, PH-meter, cm/inch ruler, measuring tape, scissors, poking tool.

- Vacuum packing.

- Proper clothes and aprons, rags and towels.

- Cleaning and sanitizing equipment.

- First aid kit.

RECIPES

ATRIAUX

This is the first sausage made on the spot and grilled, ready to be eaten by the crew who does the butchering job. It is taken home by all the members of the family or the visitors to be eaten the next day.

30 %	Liver
35 %	Heart, spleen, lungs, kidney
35 %	50/50, head trimmings
100 %	

1.50 %	Salt and cure
0.50 %	Sugar
6.00 %	Fresh herbs (parsley, chives, marjoram, onion, shallot)
2.00 %	Wine
0.50 %	Spices (pepper, allspice)

Trim liver from veins.
Grind 5 mm, add ingredients, (Herbs coarsely chopped) and blend thoroughly.
Wrap a handful in cowl fat to form a small bundle.
Refrigerate, they will keep for about a week.

Bake or grill for serving.

BOUDIN NOIR

There are many ways of making a blood sausage. Many incorporate fillers (lean and fat or cereals like rice). This one is clean and delicate with the consistency of flan, (crème caramel).

43 %	Pork blood
43 %	Whole milk
9 %	Lard
5 %	Yellow onions
100 %	

1.60 %	Salt
0.15 %	Pepper
0.10 %	Nutmeg
0.10 %	Marjoram
0.05 %	Cinnamon
0.10 %	Hydrolyzed proteins (Maggi aroma, aminos, soy sauce)

- At collection the blood has to be whipped for a couple of minutes, to prevent coagulation (the fibers of the clotting fibrin will accrete on the whip) and quickly refrigerated.
- Stir and screen the blood. Warm to 85 ° F, watch to avoid coagulation.
- Melt the lard, add chopped onions roasted to blond.
- Mix in warm blood and warmed up milk. To form an emulsion the mixing of blood milk and fat, must occur at the warmest temperature possible, without coagulating the blood proteins up to 110°F.
- Add spices and lard and onions.
- Cream can be added to the milk for a richer texture.
- Funnel liquid into beef middle casing, tie at desired length.
- Cook in180° F water for 30-50 minutes. This will set (coagulate) the "boudin" as very delicate custard. It will firm up when cold.
- Refrigerate and keep for a couple of weeks.

Sauté or bake and serve with apple compote and sautéed onions or mashed potatoes.

If you have only access to the frozen commercial blood, beware that it contains 20 to 30% water, is pre-salted and partially coagulated. We managed to get a decent "boudin", by, first, breaking the clots in the chopper at high speed, then, replacing part of the milk with NFDM in the chopper, before warming the mix.

RILLETTES

Baking Rillettes is a very French tradition, it corresponds to a simple, very old, way of preserving the meat, essentially dehydrating the proteins and protecting them with the melted fat, while developing mouth watering aromas and taste in a fine, spreadable form.

Use pure pork meat in it natural proportion of fat, about one third, from mature pork. Other meats from fat poultry can also be used in combination.
A similar technique is used for the production of "confits" of goose or duck.

100 %	Pork meat 1/3 fat like CT Butt or Belly
1.50 %	Salt (cure is optional)
0.15 %	Black Pepper

The meat can be pre-cured overnight in order to improve color and flavor.

Cut the lean in about 100g pieces and the fat in quite smaller pieces to facilitate the melting. It is even better to grind the fat.
The slow cooking is best done in large cookers or for smaller batch in cast iron pots with fitting lid.

- First render the fat, then, roast the meat pieces.
- A refinement consists of adding cut marrow bones at this stage to improve the flavor and texture with the marrow.
- Pack the meat, add the salt and set the lid on the cooking pot. The natural juice needs to cover the meat, if not add some broth, don't swamp, remember the purpose is to evaporate the water.
- The fat will concentrate on top. Steam must still escape slowly to concentrate the broth.
- Simmer at about 200° F until the fat is clear on top, the fat pieces and the meat completely soft, when fibers can be easily separated.
- Eventually discard the bones, separate the cooked meats, from the fat and separately the leftover cooking broth.
- In a bowl with spatula by hand or better in a mixer start crushing the meat.
- Add the pepper.
- As needed incorporate, first the cooking broth set aside then part of the fat to achieve the desired texture. Keep the mass at about 120° F.

- Pick the occasional vein or gristle and discard.
- Pack small containers When you achieve the desired texture and consistency. The French use individual crocks of stoneware, to allow for quick consumption after opening.
- Cover the top of the rillettes with the very hot fat. This lid of lard acts as a barrier and will keep the meat with reduced water content, even without refrigeration for several weeks, until opened.

In France Rillettes appear on the table before the meal is served. They are spread on the Baguette, like we, here, use butter, but for a much greater taste. It makes you enjoy the local wine more than any Chateau Mouton Rothschild by itself.

PATE DE CAMPAGNE

40 %	Fresh liver, veins removed.
15 %	Butt fat
30 %	Pork 70/30
<u>15 %</u>	Belly straps
100 %	

1.60 %	Salt (cure is optional)
0.30 %	Ground black pepper
0.10 %	Garlic powder
0.30 %	Allspices
0.70 %	Armagnac, Cognac or brandy

- Trim liver from major gall and blood veins, they get very hard when cooked.
- Poach both fats in boiling water 5 minutes, drip and cool.
- Grind fat and lean trimmings at 5 mm.
- Grind liver at 10 mm.
- In bowl-mixer, blend fat, lean and spices for one minute.
- Then add liver and blend 3 minutes, let the paste temperature raise to 60-65° F, add liquor in finale.
- Fill mold garnished with "bardière" (thin sheet of back fat), cover with cowl fat.
- Bake in oven 250°F to 150°F at core. The baking temperature and time controls the degree of rendering and flavor and texture development that ingredients demand and you prefer.
- When done pour a hot strong and flavored aspic to flush the excess melted fat then refrigerate. Uncut "pâté" will keep 2-3 weeks
- You can decorate the top and glaze over with more aspic after refrigeration.

Charcutier. Salumiere. Wurstmeister.

PATE EN CROUTE

There are no limits to your fancy to use all kind of force-meat and marinated "lèches" for the core of the filling. Emulsions, sausages, pâtés, all pastes can be used as force-meat alone or in combination.

The purpose of the "lèches" is to get a marking of the slice with different color textures and tastes.

To get started you can make a meat pie, with a simple sausage filling.

It is also a great way of valorizing left over paste.

The baking temperature and time controls the degree of rendering and flavor and texture development that ingredients demand and you prefer.

This is where your creative talents will find their most refined expression.

For the crust make a "pâte brisée":

55 %	All-purposes flour
28 %	Lard softened and whipped
5 %	Egg
1 %	Salt
2 %	Sugar
9 %	Ice water
100%	

- Roll the dough to garnish the mold, (preferably articulated if rectangular; round, conical work well too.
- Fill and pack inside the dhow with your selected meats, you may want to partially pre-cook the "lèches" to reduce the shrinkage, while baking.
- Cover and close with the dough.
- Pinch the edges tightly.
- Leave an open row on top, or punch out vents to release the steam.
- Bake at 300°F. Vary the temperature to find the balance between the crust crispness and the inside texture.
- Drain the fat if there is a lot of rendering.
- Refrigerate overnight.
- Fill, in a few repeated steps, with liquid (warm) flavored aspic after cooling.

After thorough refrigeration, use a serrated knife to slice the crust of the pâté; serve with "cornichons".

162

"GELEE", ASPIC

It will be used to soak the "pâtés", when they come out of the oven, to glaze, or as a delicate and delicious garnish around cold cuts.

100 %	Skins, feet, bones
5.00 %	Onions, "bouquet-garni", celery, carrots
1.00 %	Salt

- Simmer in large pot for 12 hours.
- Set aside the skins after 2 1/2 hours, if used in sausage recipes. See COTECHINO, ZAMPONE, SKIN-BLOCK.
- Skim, as needed the foam during cooking.
- When done, drain the stock to be clarified as aspic.
- Set aside solids.
- Reduce the clarified stock, to the desired strength.
- Flavor the aspic with Armagnac or Cognac and some hydrolyzed proteins, like Aminos, Maggi aroma or soy sauce.
- The cold set aspic need to be firm to touch.
- After cooling, separate bones and gristle from meats and skin. The meat and gelatinous part can be used as base ingredient for a delicious "ragu".

SKIN-BLOCK

"Schwartenblock" in German is an indispensable complement in many sausage formulation; it adds juiciness, since skins processed this way are a source of collagen.

100 %   Pre-cooked skins (trimmed of fat)

1.00 %   Salt
10.00 %   Ice or stock

- Grind 3 mm, still warm or cold.
- In bowl-chopper, add ice or liquid, blend into a very sticky cream.
- Transfer to container and refrigerate. Overnight it will form a very rubbery block.
- Cut and grind 3 mm to ad as an ingredient to desired formula.

Ground skin-block can be added to nearly everything, when juiciness is required. Resist the devil's temptation to use it as a substitute for meat to lower your cost and sacrifice quality.

CRACKLINGS, (CICCILOLI, CRETONS, GRATONS LYONAIS)

Actually the main product is the LARD; the most under-valued source of clean, natural and balanced cooking fat.

100 %	Leaf Lard, mesenteric fat and or fat trimmings
0.50 %	Salt
	Twigs of Rosemary

- Dice the fat coarsely finger-size or grind 15 mm.
- Render the fat, first on medium heat, to boil out the water. Stir frequently to avoid burning the bottom of the pot, then let the temperature rise until the cracklings are fried and take some color.
- Separate and drain the crackling.
- Pour the lard into jars or containers, garnish with a twig of rosemary on top. Some use lard flavored with roasted onions as a substitute to butter, to spread over country bread.

To avoid the bottom burning, over an open flame, it is very effective to do the rendering in a convection oven.
Snack on cracklings, lightly salted. Use as toppings or use as ingredient in "focaccia".

MOUSSE DE FOIE (LIVER PATE), BRAUNSCHWEIGER (LIVERWURST)

What a nice way to make your own "foie-gras"; it will be a challenge to make it as smooth as silk.

30 %	Liver
20 %	Stock ("gelée")
<u>50 %</u>	"Mouilles", soft fat from the flanc
100 %	

1.50 %	Salt and cure I; *you remember what we discussed p. 118 CURING.*
0.10 %	Pepper
0.10 %	Cardamom
0.50 %	Cognac
0.05 %	Garlic Powder
1.00 %	Roasted onions
2.00 %	Non fat dry milk (emulsifier)

- Grind, salt and reduce in chopper the liver into a soft paste, hold it refrigerated.
- Poach the fat in boiling water or stock for 5-10min, drain.
- Emulsify the hot fat in chopper with the stock and the emulsifier, salt and spices.
- Incorporate the prepared liver, when the temperature is below 110° F.
- Stuff it into casing or in "terrine" mold.
- Cook to 150° F internally (steam at 180° F or "bain-marie" at 195° F).

The "mousse de foie" is served cold, often garnished with diced aspic.
It can be used as marking, instead of "lèches" in a "pâté en croute".

KNAGI

With a Baguette and some Mustard, it is the old fashion 10 O'clock snack of the "charcutier", hot from the kettle, in the kitchen, while it is sold hot in the shop, as the specialty of the day.

100 %   Snout, lips, ears (inside cartilage removed) and tail, bone in or boneless, clean and devoid of hair.

- Burn the remaining hair, over an open soft flame, no torch; shave clean for a finishing touch.
- Brine for 2-3 days at 50° F (extend time if cooler).
- Cook for 2 ½ H until skin is soft in stock from the bones and skins (GELEE, ASPIC).
- Pull from bones and serve hot.

KNAGI is further processed into HEADCHEESE.

TROTTERS can be prepared the same way.

Brine :   Ratio: brine/meat = 2/1
Water   1.000 g or 1 liter   *It is the same!*
            Salt   100 g
            Sugar   50 g
            Cure   10 g pink salt, or better 2 g nitrate
            Non-acid starter culture
            "Bouquet garni" optional.
            Bay leave, rosemary, pepper, allspice, coriander, etc.

HEADCHEESE

Why is collagen facial cream a luxury item and headcheese, the best source of collagen, a neglected nutritional treasure?

100 %   Boneless snout, lips, cheek and tongue, (ears optional because of the cartilage).

Broth pices: Shallot, bay, rosemary, pepper, clove.
Blending spices: Pepper, nutmeg, allspice, cinnamon, "Marsala" wine.

- Clean and burn remaining hairs.
- Brine the ingredients as in KNAGI.
- Cook in stock till skin is tender.
- Tongues need to be peeled after cooking.
- Cut as julienne or grind using a very large plate, no less than 25 mm.
- Blend with spices and "Marsala" wine.
- Mix 1/3 concentrated stock and 2/3 meats.
- Stuff into large, caliber 100-120, casing.
- Pasteurize at 160° F if you need to extend the shelf life beyond a couple of weeks.

Cooking needs to release enough gelatin, to bind and set the mix, when refrigerated, to be sliceable. Best to cook the heads for 2-3 H into a previously simmered stock made of bones, skin and trotters. (See GELEE, ASPIC).

SALSICCIA

The ingredients, here, shall not contain any soft fat, to avoid rendering.
Mild and aromatic, meaty sausage to grill or to be used as garnish, topping or stuffing.

30 %	Pork II
45 %	Pork 70/30
15 %	Butt fat, back fat or belly straps
<u>10 %</u>	Water
100 %	

1.50 %	Salt
0.20 %	Pepper
0.10 %	Nutmeg
0.02 %	Clove
0.03 %	Cinnamon
0.05 %	Rosemary
0.05 %	Sage
1.00 %	Hydrolyzed proteins, bouillon extract, etc.
	Non-acid starter culture

- Chill or best lightly freeze the meat at 28 ° F.

- Grind with a 4 mm plate.

- Add water and mix carefully to avoid smearing, until bound; cool again if need be.
- Stuff it into sheep casing 24/26 mm, or equivalent collagen.
- Keep as coil, or twist to size.
- Braid by 3 in 10 cm links to make **CHIPOLATA**.

SAUCISSE A ROTIR

This is a Swiss sausage from the canton of Vaud, a Brat type, which is best cooked, starting with a little white wine at the bottom of the pan, covered until evaporated and then browned. The ingredients include soft fat, which will render and yield delicious gravy.

45 %	Pork II
25 %	Soft belly straps
15 %	Back-fat
<u>15 %</u>	Water
100 %	

1.50 %	Salt
0.20 %	Pepper
0.10 %	Nutmeg
0.20 %	Marjoram
1.00 %	White wine like Chablis

- Refrigerate well the meats, almost frozen.
- Grind using the 3.5 mm plate.
- Add water as needed, mix well, the paste will form some emulsion, to hold it from smearing, use up to 3 % non-fat dry-milk.
- Stuff it into pork-middle casing 28/30, or 30/32 mm.
- Coil or twist to link size.

This formulation, with the soft fat, will form some emulsion, the art is to have enough good meat proteins to hold the emulsion water based and not invert into smear. Highly binding and water absorbing NFDM can substitute muscle lean.
50/50 trim with 3% NFDM and up to 20% water, will yield a very good **BREAKFAST SAUSAGE** if you add a touch of sage to the spices.

FLEISCHKAESE, LEBERKAESE

This is the most popular meat preparation in the "Schwabenland" of southern Germany. It is a baked pure meat loaf, served in slices as cold cut, or in thick slice for grilling. It can be cubed or julienned, served cold or grilled to replace the ubiquitous chicken breast.

30 %	Pork II
30 %	Pork 70/30
20 %	Back-fat
20 %	Ice flakes
100 %	
	Options:
10 %	Skin-block (add juiciness).
5 %	Pork liver adds color and flavor.

1.50 %	Salt and cure
0.50 %	Sugar or Lactose
0.50 %	Onions
0.25 %	Pepper
0.10 %	Nutmeg
0.05 %	Coriander
0.10 %	Paprika
0.02 %	Ginger
0.02 %	Caraway

The emulsion is made in the chopper in four steps: the respect of temperature is critical:

- All the lightly frozen meat and all the salt, chop until 32° F.
- Adding half the Ice, chop until 40° F, to build a very strong and smooth paste.
- Add the fat, the spices and the onions, chop until 46° F.
- Add the rest of the ice, chop until 53° F, temperature of strongest emulsion binding.
- Fill the baking forms.
- Glaze with water and score the surface.
- Bake initially at 250° F, to brown the top then reduce to 170° F, until 150° F at the core.

Charcutier. Salumiere. Wurstmeister.

KALBSBRATWURST, BOCKWURST

This is a Swiss specialty from St-Gall, made of veal and pork with milk. It is excellent too, if made only with pork meat.
They are eaten grilled or browned, served with "rösti" (hash brown) and caramelized onions.

35 %	Veal or pork I
10 %	Pork 70/30
25 %	Butt or jowl fat
<u>30 %</u>	Milk, preferably frozen in flakes
100 %	

1.70 %	Salt
0.20 %	Pepper
0.15 %	Allspice
0.10 %	Cardamom
0.10 %	Lemon peel

The emulsion is made in the chopper in 4 steps; the respect of temperature is critical:

- All the lightly frozen meat and all the salt, chop until 32° F.
- Adding half the Milk, chop to 40° F until very smooth paste.
- Add all the fat and spices, chop until 46° F.
- Add the rest of the milk, chop until 53° F.
- Stuff into pork-middle casing 30-32mm, twist into links.
- Blanch in water at 170° F, for 20-25 minutes until firm.
- Cool in ice water.

SMOKIE (SCHWEINSWURST)

This is a very versatile and tasty slim sausage. It can be enjoyed as a cold finger food, served as a better hotdog in a bun or grilled.

20 %	Lean beef (hamburger)
05 %	Pork fat II
03 %	Skin block
05 %	Ice flakes
67 %	Pork 70/30
100 %	

1.50 %	Salt and cure II
0.10 %	Pepper
0.10 %	Nutmeg
0.10 %	Coriander
0.05 %	Caraway
0.10 %	Hydrolyzed proteins (soy sauce, liquid amino, Maggi aroma)

- Grind beef and skin block using the 3 mm plate.
- Emulsify all the beef and skin block with ice and all the salt, then pork fat II. Follow the 4 steps procedure, (FLEISCHKAESE).
- When smooth incorporate the Pork 70/30 previously ground at 5 mm and blend in without further chopping.
- Add spices.
- Stuff into sheep casing 26-28 mm.
- Smoke at 120° F.
- Cook at 170° F 20-25' until 150° F at core.
- Shower to cool.

FRANKFURTER

This is the real thing. The sausage will shrivel a little, get plump when heated, and snap when bitten.

20 %	Pork II
30 %	Pork 70/30
30 %	Pork trimmings 50/50
<u>20 %</u>	Ice flakes
100 %	

1.50 %	Salt and cure II
0.20 %	Pepper
0.10 %	Nutmeg
0.05 %	Coriander
0.05 %	Ginger

	Options:
0.30 %	Polyphosphates to be used with frozen meat
	Non-acid starter culture

- Emulsify in 4 stages as specified in FLEISCHKAESE. See EMULSION, pages 99 and 106.
- Stuff in small (26-28 mm) pork middle casing, twist in 4 oz. links, hangs on smoking sticks.
- Hang to dry cure and smoke lightly.
- Cook at 170° F until 150° F at core.
- Shower to cool; the water chills the sausage rapidly, reduces the evaporation shrinkage and shrinks the casing, thus adding to the "knack" bite.

SAUCISSON DE LYON A CUIRE (SAUCISSE DE MORTEAU)

Masterpiece of the "charcutier", this sausage is lightly fermented, made to be cooked, but can be dried as well. The slow curing and fermenting in natural casing makes it a remarkable sausage.

In Lyon it is flavored either with pistachios or truffle. It is stuffed in beef casing and not smoked; in Morteau, it is stuffed in chitterling casings, clipped by a wood spike and cold smoked with fir wood.

In France the "saucisson" is usually not refrigerated and is cooked by the consumer to be served hot. It is preferable to pre-cook it for the US consumer.

65 %	Pork I
35 %	Jowl or butt fat
100 %	

1.70 %	Salt and cure, preferably saltpeter @ 0.03%
0.25 %	Sugar
0.20 %	Pepper
0.10 %	Garlic fresh
0.50 %	Port or sherry
	Starter culture non-acid
	Options:
0.50 %	Pistachios
0.20 %	Black truffle slices or dried morels.

- Pre size the meat and fat for easy grinding.
- Refrigerate the lean and lightly freeze the fat.
- Mix lean and fat and grind using the 5 mm or 8 mm plate, careful not to smear.
- Mix thoroughly with all the ingredients, until a solid binding is achieved; refrigerate before or after if need be.

It is less risky to use the chopper to reduce meat and fat to size, at low blade and bowl speed and to initiate the mixing at the blade low speed and high bowl speed.

- Stuff it into large (60 mm) beef casings. (Truffles slices are inserted in the casing, prior stuffing to show on the inside of the casing)
- Cure and dry in fermenting room for 24-48 hours at 70° F.
- Mature at room temperature for a few days; expect to shrink about 10 to 15 %.
- Cook at 170° F to 155° F at core.

Charcutier. Salumiere. Wurstmeister.

MORTADELLA DI FEGATO

It is a delicious sausage, with a very complex flavor, which excel as a cold appetizer.
Like the "saucisson de Lyon" it is a semi-fermented sausage to which pork liver is incorporated.

40 %	Pork II
30 %	Pork 70/30
20 %	Back-fat
10 %	Pork liver
100 %	

1.80 %	Salt and cure, preferably saltpeter @ 0.03 %
0.30 %	Sugar
0.20 %	Pepper
0.05 %	Allspice
0.05 %	Cinnamon
0.03 %	Thyme
0.10 %	Cognac
	Non-acid forming starter culture

Use the same technique as for the "SAUCISSON DE LYON".
On page 23 see how the "fidighella" is bound in a circle to distinguish from "salame".

COTECHINO

Rich in gelatin, from the boiled pork skins, a slowly cooked "cotechino" will make your lips stick. "Cotechino" together with beef, tongue, hen and "testina" (blanched veal head), compose the meats of the famous Italian "bollito misto", served with the equally famous "salsa verde".
It is also delectable, by itself, when served with lentils and steamed potatoes.

50 %	Pork II (or 50/50 Pork/Beef)
25 %	Back-fat
25 %	Pork skin, preferably thin, raw or pre-boiled.
100 %	

1.80 %	Salt and cure, preferably saltpeter @ 0.03 %
0.20 %	Pepper
0.05 %	Cinnamon
0.05 %	Garlic fresh
0.03 %	Clove
0.20 %	Wine
	Non-acid starter culture

- Slightly freeze the skins if pre-cooked and grind with 3 mm plate; do it twice, first at 10 mm if using fresh skins.
- Mix the ground skin with the meat, fat and grind with 3.5 mm plate.
- Mix with salt spices and wine until bound.
- Stuff in Beef Middles 55 mm.
- Tie in 10-12 oz links.
- Hang to cure in moderately humid 70° F, for 2 days.
- Mature at room temperature for a few days; expect to shrink about 10 to 15 %.
- Keep refrigerated.

If made with raw skins, the "cotechino", needs to be simmered for, at least, a couple of hours to convert the collagen of the skin into gelatin before serving.

ZAMPONE

The original recipe requires the skin of the fore trotter of the pig, which needs to be carefully peeled from the leg without any cutting and thoroughly defatted for the paste to adhere.

The USDA, sometimes, requires from packers to cut out the skin between the fingers, the trotter can be left in place as tip of the "zampone". In this case the longer and bulkier fore leg can be wrapped in cloth and bound in order to obtain a regular shape for cooking.

An alternate simplified way is to cut a rectangle of skin, wide as the circumference and long as the intended casing, (60-70 mm); the skin is garnished inside the casing. While stuffing make sure to push the skin to contact the inside of the casing.

- For stuffing use the "COTECHINO" paste.
- Follow the raw skin curing and cooking method.
- Stich the skin to close tightly, or use the cloth.

Most recipes call for less skins and added whole eggs to the paste. "Zampone" is a noble sausage, which requires a lot of labor and care and is part of the Christmas table. It is traditionally served with lentils.

MORTADELLA

What makes the "mortadella" such a special sausage is the process, which removes water from the meat and allows for some fermentation while warming up in the oven. It has to be a large sausage. Very large is even better, because it slows down the baking. Cheap version incorporate pork tripe and skins, here we make the noblest pure meat kind.

40 %	Pork II
35 %	Pork 50/50
15 %	Jowls cubed ½ "
<u>10 %</u>	Ice flakes
100 %	

1.50 %	Salt and cure II, preferably saltpeter @ 0.03 %
0.30 %	Sugar
0.20 %	Broken pepper
0.10 %	Coriander ground
0.10 %	Coriander whole
0.05 %	Rosemary
0.20 %	Sherry
0.50 %	Shelled pistachios (optional)
	Non-acid starter culture

- Wash the "lardelli" (diced jowl) to remove the surface oil with hot water, and refrigerate.
- Grind the meats with 3 mm plate and slightly freeze.
- In the bowl-chopper, chop the meats with all the salt to 32° F.
- Add the ice and chop to 40° F.
- Add the spices and wine, withhold the whole coriander and pistachios, and chop to 55° F.
- In the mixer add the "lardelli", the pistachios and coriander; blend until the "lardelli" stick to the paste.
- If you use saltpeter and starters, let the paste rest overnight.
- Stuff the paste into large collagen or fibrous casing or bladder.
- Tie to hang with solid twine and loop.
- Step-bake in oven:

- With damper open, progressively and slowly raise the temperature to 140° F.
- Closing damper, raise the oven temperature to 180° F / core temperature of 155° F.
- Cool the "mortadella" in a ventilated room without showering.

The process is meant to evaporate part of the water; it reduces the water activity and improves the shelf life substantially.

LANDJAEGER

That is the German for hunter as in "Cacciatore". A convenient pocket sized dry-sausage with a lot of character.

80 %	Beef lean or sow lean
20 %	Back-fat
100 %	

2.50 %	Salt and cure II, preferably saltpeter @ 0.03 %
0.50 %	Sugar
0.10 %	Pepper
0.10 %	Coriander
0.30 %	Broken caraway
0.10 %	Garlic powder
0.50 %	Red wine
	Starter culture high-acid

- Break down the lightly frozen lean, during 4-5 rounds on the chopper.
- Add the fat.
- Reduce the final size to 3 mm.
- Add the spices, the wine and starter.
- Mix until tacky without smearing.
- Stuff into pork-middle in sections of two equal, twisted links of 4-5 oz.
- Flatten the links and fold the casing ends over the links. This is best done using a mold (It can be easily done with a piece of 4x2" of proper length into which the two opposite shapes are gouged with a 15 mm router bit).
- When shaped, lay parallel, side-by-side on a sheet-pan.
- Stack the filled sheet-pans, cover with an empty sheet-pan and press down.
- Lay in cooler for 3-5 days, until cured.
- Hang the pairs over a smoking stick and cold smoke.
- Let dry at room temperature for 1-2 weeks.
- If grinding, use the 3 mm plate and mix thoroughly.

SAUCISSE SECHE (DRY SAUSAGE)

Here is a simple recipe. Try other meats: goat, lamb, donkey, turkey, ostrich, alligator, etc. and create the flavor to your taste. Any lean fresh meat, in combination with the pork fat will work.

50 %	Beef lean, or any other lean meat
30 %	Pork 70/30
<u>20 %</u>	Back-fat
100 %	

2.50 %	alt and Cure II, preferably saltpeter @ 0.03 %
0.50 %	Sugar
0.20 %	Pepper
0.05 %	Nutmeg
0.15 %	Garlic fresh
	Starter culture salami low-temp. - low-acid

- Break down the lightly frozen lean, during 4-5 rounds on the chopper.
- Add the fat.
- Reduce the final size to 3mm adding the spices, the wine and starter.
- Mix well until tacky and bound without smearing.
- Stuff it into pork middles 34-36.
- Twist in one-foot long links.
- Tie or knot both end of the link chain
- Roll the attached links over a smoking stick.
- Ferment at 70° F for 2-3 days, starting with a humid air.
- Dry at 55-60° F, RH 75-80% for a couple of weeks. Drying in a cooler will take a bit longer.

CACCIATORE, SALAMETTO, SALAMELLA, SECCHI, STROLGHINO, ETC.

Italians expect this popular type of small salami to be mellow, mild and very aromatic. Contrary to his larger brethren, which mature more slowly, the "cacciatore" is meant to be eaten within a few weeks.

It is typically served whole on a cutting board with bread and wine, as "antipasto", while you wait for your main dish, may be a risotto, enjoyed sitting in the shade of an old chestnut tree at a granite table and bench on the shore of an Italian lake.

---

55 %	Pork I hand trimmed and de-sinewed
30 %	Pork belly or Pork 70/30
<u>15 %</u>	Back-fat
100 %	

2.50 %	Salt and cure II, preferably saltpeter @ 0.03 %
0.50 %	Sugar
0.10 %	Black pepper ground
0.10 %	Black pepper broken
0.20 %	Garlic fresh
0.50 %	Red wine
	Low-acid starter culture

- Cut the meats and fat to a size smaller than the nozzle of the grinder.
- Spread on sheets to allow some drying.
- Freeze the lean lightly @ 28° F, and freeze the fat at 15° F.
- Grind using a 5mm plate for "nostrano" or 3.5 mm for "Milano" style, making sure that the meats transit the grinder without smearing, in order to retain the particle definition.
- Mix with the spices, starter and the wine until binding well, careful not to let the paste warm up and smear.
- The paste can also be chopped and mixed to size in the bowl-chopper.
- Pack the paste, refrigerate for one or two days.
- Stuff into pork-middles 36-38.
- Tie links of 6-8 oz. in chains of six, with a hanging loop.
- Hang the chains on a smoking stick.

- Initiate the fermenting, raising the temperature to 70° F in high humidity for about 8 hours.
- Change the air and start drying, with cycles of short drying down to 60-65%, then letting the salami rest and the RH go back to 85-88%. Repeat the cycle while the temperature is dropped progressively to 55-60° F.
- After a week the salami will finish drying at 75-80% and 55° F
- I like it best when it has shrunk about 25 %.

CRESPONE (SAUCISSON SEC PUR PORK)

This is the Italian name of the chitterling, or large intestine, which has a willowy and contorted shape. It is a bit difficult to stuff but nothing else come close to developing the perfect aroma of the "salame".

75 %	Pork I
25 %	Jowl or butt fat
100 %	

2.50 %	Salt and cure II, preferably saltpeter @ 0.03 %
0.50 %	Sugar
0.20 %	Coarsely broken black pepper
0.20 %	Garlic fresh
0.50%	Sherry wine
	Low-acid starter culture

- Cut the meats and fat to a size smaller than the nozzle of the grinder.
- Spread on sheets to allow some drying.
- Lightly freeze the lean and freeze the fat at 15° F.
- Grind using a 5 mm plate, making sure that the meat transit the grinder without smearing, in order to retain the particle definition.
- Mix with the spices, starter and the wine, get a strong binding, be careful not to let the paste warm up and smear.
- Pack the paste, refrigerate for one or two days.
- Stuff into chitterling sections, pre-tied long enough for about one pound each, slowly, move the casing left and right on the horn to fill the sides; stuff without too much pressure.
- Finish the shaping of the salami in the casing by hand.
- Close tie the loose-end, the "crespone" comes pre-tied with a hanging loop. If convenient you can form chains of desired length.
- Hang on a stick.
- Ferment, dry and age.

Refer to FERMENTING, DRYING AND AGING page 126

Charcutier. Salumiere. Wurstmeister.

ROSETTE DE LYON, FELINO, GENTILE, SALCHICHON DE VICH

Every European sub-culture considers sausages stuffed in the pork-after casing (prosaically the rectum), to be the best. Only selected meats and fat are allowed in the recipes.

This fat and sturdy casing is very slow to dry and impart extraordinary flavor and texture to the product.

75 %	Pork I, traditionally all the trimmed meat of mature heavy hogs
25 %	Jowl or Butt Fat
100%	

2.50 %	Salt and cure II, preferably saltpeter @ 0.03 %
0.50 %	Sugar
0.20 %	Coarse broken, with some whole, black pepper
0.20 %	Garlic fresh
0.50 %	Sherry wine
	low-acid tarter culture

- Cut the meats and fat to a size smaller than the nozzle of the grinder.
- Spread on sheets, pre-condition (page 82) to allow some drying.
- Lightly freeze the fat at 15°F.
- Grind using a 5 mm plate making sure that the meats transit the grinder without smearing, in order to retain the particle definition.
- Mix with the spices, starter and the wine until bound, careful not to let the paste warm up and smear.
- Pack the paste, refrigerate for one or two days.
- Stuff into the pre-tied after casing, (inverted pork rectum, about 18 " long),
- Tie and loop, then scrape to score lengthwise the outside skin of the casing with an inverted fork; this is meant to help the drying.
- Then hang on a stick.
- Ferment and dry.
- Age up to three months.

Refer to FERMENTING, DRYING AND AGING page 126.

SALAME DI MILANO

This fine salami was developed In Milan as the first industrial quality product, when mechanical refrigeration and grinders were first available at the end of the 19th century. It is a mild and delicate one, traditionally using "bindone" casing (from horses), which won't be used in this country; it can be replaced with beef middle casings, but we will loose the easy peeling and elegant shape of the "bindone".

75 %	Pork I
25 %	Back fat
100 %	

2.70 %	Salt and cure II, preferably saltpeter @ 0.03 %
0.50 %	Sugar
0.20 %	Black pepper broken
0.10 %	Garlic fresh
0.50 %	Red wine
	Low-acid starter culture

- Cut the meats and fat to a size smaller than the nozzle of the grinder.
- Spread on sheets to allow some drying.
- Lightly freeze the lean and freeze the fat at 15°F.
- The bowl-chopper can be beneficially used to reduce the size of the particle, before grinding; or, outright, to prepare the paste to the required small particle size.
- Grind with the 3.5 mm plate; this allows for a perfect particle size control, but increases the risk of smearing.
- Mix with the spices, starter and the wine until bound, careful not to let the paste warm up and smear.
- Pack the paste, refrigerate for one or two days.
- Stuff into beef casings 70-75 mm, in chubs of 2-3 pounds, the larger 90-110 mm. at 5 to 7 Lb. is popular in this country as Genoa salami.
- Tie hard with two loops lengthwise and three loops across.
- Hang two pieces tied together over the stick allowing one up to the stick and one lower, below the other salami on the other side, alternate between pairs to give more space to each salami.
- Ferment and dry.
- Mold
- Age 70-75 caliber, four to five weeks or 90-110 six to eight weeks.

Refer to FERMENT, DRY AND AGE page 126.

SALAME NOSTRANO

This coarse version is the traditional home made salami of the "Brianza", the area north of Milan, between Piemonte and Veneto, where most of today's industry was born. It is mild, but more robust in aroma and flavor than the fine "Milano" type.

55 %	Pork I
30 %	Pork belly
15 %	Back fat
100 %	

2.50 %	Salt and cure II, best with saltpeter @ 0.03 %
0.50 %	Sugar
0.20 %	Black pepper broken
0.20 %	Garlic fresh
0.50 %	Red wine
	Non-acid or low acid starter culture

- Cut the meats and fat to a size smaller than the nozzle of the grinder.
- Spread on sheets to allow some drying.
- Refrigerate the lean and freeze the fat at 15 °F.
- Mix Lean and Fat.
- Grind with the 8 mm plate, making sure that the grinder cuts well.
- Mix with the spices, starter and the wine, It will take longer to get a good binding with coarse ground meat.
- Pack the paste, refrigerate for one or two days.
- Stuff into re-sown casings 75-80 mm or beef bung, in 5-6 lb size.
- Tie very firmly with 3 or 4 lengthwise and close set cross loops.
- Ferment.
- Dry.
- Mold.
- Age for 5 to 8 weeks, depending on size.

FERMENT, DRY AND AGE as indicated page 126.

SOPRESSATA CALABRESE

This is the lifeline of the "Meridione". No life is sustainable south of Napoli without "sopressata, pane, vino, olio d'oliva e formaggio pecorino".
It has become a staple of American Italian markets, but under different shapes, pressed in Toronto or Mississauga, round and very spicy in Philadelphia.

55 %	Pork I
30 %	Pork belly
<u>15 %</u>	Back-fat
100 %	

2.50 %	Salt and cure II, best saltpeter @ 0.03 %
0.50 %	Sugar
0.15 %	Black pepper broken
0.20 %	Sweet fennel broken
0.20 %	Pepperoncini flakes
0.10 %	Garlic fresh
0.50 %	Red wine, "Meridionale", sweet and strong
	Non-acid or low acid starter culture

- Cut the meats and fat to a size smaller than the nozzle of the grinder.
- Spread on sheets to allow some drying.
- Shortly stiffen the lean and freeze the fat at 15° F.
- Grind using an 8 mm plate, making sure that the meats transit the grinder without smearing, in order to retain the particle definition. It should be no problem at this caliber.
- With spices, starter and wine, mix well enough to get a solid binding.
- Pack the paste, refrigerate for one or two days.
- Stuff into chitterlings, if to be sold as chub; use the chitterling, preferably de-nerved, to allow for a fuller shape, but it requires a very careful handling and tight binding, since the casing looses most of its strength. It retains the best aroma.
- For slicing, use large beef middles. They are preferred if the salamis are to be pressed.
- To press the salami flat, the industry uses double spring loaded mesh grates to hang the salami in the fermenting room and drying room. The salami can also be pressed with weighted boards, in the cooler, before the fermenting.
- Another way is to lay the salami flat on a grate for fermenting and turning it over for further drying.
- Ferment, dry and age.

Refer to FERMENT, DRY AND AGE page 126.

SOBRASADA, LONGANISSA

Here we speak Catalan. The "sobrasada" is a specialty of the Baleares Islands and Cataluña.

It is the name of a large soft and fatter dry sausage.

Pork and soft fat are ground very fine and form an emulsion flavored with the local peppers.

The same paste stuffed in smaller pork middle casing is called "longanissa".

50 %	Pork I
30 %	Pork 70/30
10 %	Back-fat
<u>10 %</u>	Sheet lard
100 %	

2.20 %	Salt and cure II or saltpeter @ 0.03 %
0.30 %	Sugar
0.15 %	Black pepper ground
0.15 %	Garlic fresh
0.50 %	"Pimenton dulce" or "picante", ground
	Low-acid starter culture

- Refrigerate, pre-cut and mix all the meats and fat.
- Pre-grind with a large 8 mm plate.
- Refrigerate again and refine, grinding with a 2 mm plate.
- Mix with all ingredients until smooth. The paste forms a sticky fat emulsion, actually deliberately smearing.
- Stuff into pork-bung or large beef casing, for "sobrasada".
- Stuff in pork-middle 34-36 mm, for "longanissa"; make large loops of about one foot in diameter with twine loop for hanging.
- Ferment at a low temperature, (max. 68° F) and maintain sufficient humidity to avoid crusting.
- Hardly dry, slowly; with high fat content this salami will loose only about 15 % of its weight.
- Age according to casing caliber.

The smeared texture makes this salami spreadable even after fermentation.

NDUJA

It is the "Pugliese" cousin. It is the same kind of spreadable salami, with variation in the use of local spices. The meat is fermented in bins, after the first grinding, before the second grinding and blending. It tends to develop a more acidity.

ANDOUILLE NOUVELLE ORLEANS

Interesting to observe, how the mixing of cultures, keep the same name for sausages which are quite different. French "andouilette", Louisiana Andouille and Calabrese "nduja", each are very different sausage but share the same name root, probably as ancient as the Romans. Similarly in Ticino "luganiga" Portugal "longaniza", Bulgaria "luganga", Geneva "longeole", all are distant relative to the "luccana", which was the provision of the Roman centurion.

45 %	Pork II
25 %	Pork 70/30
20 %	Back-fat
10 %	Yellow onions diced
100 %	

1.50 %	Salt and cure II
0.30 %	Sugar
0.15 %	Black pepper ground
0.10 %	Nutmeg
0.10 %	Allspice
0.20 %	Garlic fresh
0.30 %	Cayenne pepper
	Non-acid starter culture

- Pre dice and refrigerate meat and fat.
- Grind using a 5 mm plate, refrigerate, if need be.
- Mix with all ingredients until binding.
- Stuff into pork-middles.
- Link, twisting at 10 in.
- Loop pairs over smoking sticks.
- Keep cold overnight until casing dries.
- Cold-smoke for 2-3 hours
- Dry at 60-70° F and 75-80 % RH, during 2-3 days.
- The andouille needs to be cooked for serving.

SOPRESSA VENETA

No, this one is not pressed! It is very popular in the N-E of Italy. The very large size demands a rather long fermentation, which develops the aroma without much acidification. It is consumed when still young, soft and mild.

60 %	Pork I
20 %	Pork belly
<u>20 %</u>	Pork jowl or butt fat
100 %	

2.50 %	Salt and cure, preferably saltpeter @ 0.03 %
0.35 %	Sugar
0.20 %	Black pepper broken
0.20 %	Garlic fresh
0.30 %	Sweet white wine
	Low acid tarter culture

- Cut the meats and fat to a size smaller than the nozzle of the grinder.
- Spread on sheets to allow some drying.
- Lightly freeze the lean and freeze the Fat at 15° F.
- Grind with a 8 mm plate making sure that the meats transit the grinder without smearing, in order to retain the particle definition.
- Mix the spices, starter and the wine to achieve a solid binding.
- Pack the paste, refrigerate for one or two days.
- Stuff it into beef-bungs, to capacity. (8-10 Lb.)
- Tie firm with loop spaced 1 ½ ", several length running twine and double the hanging loop to secure the weight.
- Hang on a stick.
- Ferment, dry, age; refer to FERMENTING, DRYING, AGING page 126.
- In Italy the "sopressa" is consumed when the shrinkage passes 25 %.
- It is consumed still mild and soft, sliced thicker than drier salami and enjoyed in a way similar to fresh Mozzarella.

SALAME TOSCANO, LE VRAI SAUCISSON DE LYON

What characterizes this product is the softer emulsified paste with incorporated "lardelli" or "lardons". It gives a mortadella look to the slices.
The large salami requires a long aging.

50 %	Pork I
20 %	Pork II
10 %	Soft fat ("mouilles" or leaf lard)
10 %	Washed cubed back fat
100 %	

2.50 %	Salt and cure, preferably saltpeter @ 0.03 %
0.50 %	Sugar
0.15 %	Black pepper ground
0.10 %	Nutmeg
0.20 %	Garlic fresh
0.50 %	Red wine
	Low-acid starter culture

- The "lardelli" must be diced, washed shortly in hot water to remove the surface oil and refrigerated, prior to the preparation of the paste.
- The paste is made in the chopper.
- Slightly freeze the meat.
- Grind the soft fat with a 3 mm plate and set aside.
- Chop the lean meats to a fine paste with particles still visible.
- Add the soft fat to the lean and emulsify it; do not let the temperature raise above 50° F.
- Add the ingredients with the wine and starters to the paste
- Mix in the "lardelli", making sure they stick into the paste.
- Stuff it into beef bung to capacity (8-10 lb).
- Hang the salami for 24-48 H in cooler to cure.
- Ferment and dry.
- Age for about two months; be very cautious not to crust this delicate salami.

Refer to FERMENT, DRY AND AGE page 126.

FINOCCHIONA

This salami from Florence exist in two versions, one, which we propose here is made in a classic way, the slice holds the fat, the paste is well coagulated it is mild with a strong sweet fennel accent. It may be a little tangy.

What the local prefer is the variety, which they call "sbricciolona" the difference is due to a deliberate lack of coagulation of the paste, resulting from reduced blending and reduced lactic fermentation; it develops instead a somewhat crumbling texture and a characteristic stronger aroma, which is balanced by the fennel.

50 %	Pork I
30 %	Pork belly
20 %	Back-fat
100 %	

2.50 %	Salt and cure, preferably saltpeter @ 0.03 %
0.50 %	Sugar
0.20 %	Black pepper broken
0,30 %	Sweet fennel partially broken
0,10 %	Garlic fresh
0,30 %	Wine
	Low-acid starter culture

- Cut the meats and fat to a size smaller than the nozzle of the grinder.
- Spread on sheets to allow some drying.
- Refrigerate the lean and freeze the Fat at 15° F.
- Mix lean and fat.
- Grind using a 8 mm plate, making sure that knife and plate cut well.
- Mix with the spices, starter and the wine until a solid binding is achieved without smear.
- Pack the paste, refrigerate for one or two days.
- Stuff it in large re-sown casing, caliber 100/120 mm (8-10 lb).
- Tie firm, with loops at 1" and 4-6 runners, doubled hanging loop.
- Then hang on a stick.
- Ferment and dry.
- Age gently, very large "finocchiona" can take more than six months to fully mature.

Refer to FERMENT, DRY AND AGE page 126.

FUET

It is a simple dry sausage, from Cataluña. It is fully cured but hardly fermented, fast drying is how it becomes shelf stable, it typically shrivels.
It is very mild with lots of aroma.

33 %	Pork I
33 %	Pork II
<u>34 %</u>	Pork belly
100 %	

2.80 %	Salt and cure, definitely saltpeter @ 0.03 %
0.20 %	Black pepper ground
0.20 %	Garlic fresh
0.50 %	Wine
	Non-acid starter culture

- Cut the meats and fat to a size smaller than the nozzle of the grinder.
- Spread on sheets to allow some drying.
- Refrigerate the lean and freeze at 15 °F.
- Mix lean and fat.
- Grind at 5 mm making sure that the grinder cuts well.
- Mix with the spices, starter and the wine, until well bound, careful not to smear.
- If needed refrigerate before stuffing pork middle 32-34 mm.
- Tie long loops of 12" to hang over the smoke stick, or simply roll a firm stuffed casing in twisted long loops over the stick.
- Hang to dry without the humid fermenting phase, beginning at 65° F and RH 75-80 %.
- The PH will stay at about PH6, but the aW (water activity value) will drop rapidly to .9 or below.
- The "fuet" characteristic is the absence of much fermentation, other than the nitrate reduction and curing (no sugar is provided). Instead fast drying is stopping the bacterial activity
- "Fuet" is enjoyed quite dry.

CHORIZO SORIA

"Pimenton de la Vera dulce" is a Spanish smoked and mild paprika, it gives to this chorizo a fabulous flavor. The texture, with very large pieces of ham, is typical of the best Spanish specialties.
Paprika limits the binding and demands a particular processing.

60 %	Pork I from the leg
20 %	Pork I
<u>20 %</u>	Pork Jowl or butt fat
100 %	

2.50 %	Salt and cure, preferably saltpeter @ 0.03 %
0.30 %	Sugar
0.15 %	Black pepper broken
0.15 %	Garlic fresh
0.50 %	"Pimenton de la Vera dulce"
0.30 %	Sherry wine
	Low-acid starter cultures

- Dice the Leg lean into ½" to 1 " size, spread and refrigerate.
- Cut the fat to pieces fit for the grinder and lightly freeze.
- Grind fat at 8mm, or chop to size in the bowl chopper.
- Cut the pork I to grinder size and lightly freeze.
- Grind the pork at 3 mm.
- Blend the ground pork I in the bowl chopper or food processor, add first 1/3 of the salt and sugar then the wine.
- When the particles are no longer visible and the paste is still at or below 45° F, add all the "pimenton".
- Mix to blend, until a good binding is reached, both type of meat with the fat and the rest of the ingredients, make sure that the fat particles are well distributed and the dice fully incorporated by the paste.
- Refrigerate.
- Stuff in beef middles 75-80 mm. or even better in de-nerved Chitterlings
- Tie in 12" chubs.
- Ferment, dry and age.

Refer to FERMENT, DRY AND AGE page 126.

CHINESE SAUSAGE, LOP CHONG

Sweet sour, often spicy are the characters differentiating the oriental dry sausages. This one also has a peculiar appearance.

40 %	Pork I
30 %	Pork II
<u>30 %</u>	Back-fat
100 %	

2.50 %	Salt and cure II, or saltpeter @ 0.03 %
2.00 %	Sugar
0.20 %	Black pepper ground
0.30 %	Garlic fresh
0.30 %	Hoisin sauce
	Low-acid starter culture

- Cut the meats to the grinder nozzle size, spread and lightly freeze.
- Dice the back-fat to ½" size, wash with hot water, to remove the surface oil, then spread to dry and refrigerate.
- Grind the lean meats with the 3 mm plate.
- Mix the ingredients and the diced fat in the lean meat until the paste sticks together.
- Refrigerate to 40° F.
- Stuff it in pork middle 36-38 mm and twist 8" links.
- Hang over smoke stick.
- Start the curing, fermenting and drying at 80 F with 85% RH and progressively reduce the temperature while drying without crusting the casing. Finish the drying in the cooler.

JAMBON ROYAL

Unlike the 3 days injected ham of the industry, here is a ham curing slowly, without water and tasting of real meat, not the watery, jellified and flavored common varieties, but also much less salty than the old fashion Virginia type.

100 %	Pork boneless long leg

2.50 %	Salt and cure, definitely, saltpeter @ 0.03 %
0.50 %	Sugar
0.50 %	Pepper, rosemary, allspice, ginger… as you like
	Non-acid starter culture

We use a boneless long leg (sirloin included), after removing topside, all the bones and shank, we keep all the muscles of the outside of the leg closely attached together with the trimmed fat and skin on the outside. It demands great precision and care in the boning and trimming of the leg.

The video THE ART AND PHILOSOPHY OF PRODUCING QUALITY PORK PRODUCTS, as well as the PowerPoint pictures of the Pork Break in http://www.francoisvecchio.com give step by step directions to that specific trim.

- In a proper container, rub the trimmed ham with all the salt, sugar, ingredients and starter culture.
- Lay the ham on the meat side down, cover with a lid.
- Set in the cooler for about two week, every 2-3 days flip the ham around, pouring the brine on top; one can shorten or lengthen the time in function of the size and thickness of the ham; the meat temperature also influences the speed of salt absorbing (colder = slower).
- Note that the salt will penetrate through the muscles but not through the skin and fat.
- The curing will firm up the meat and release brine, which is discarded at this time.
- Lay again the ham, on the meat side down, in the container and let it equalize the curing salt in the cooler for another period, equal in time to the salting duration.

- *The duration of the process of salting time and equalizing equal time can be roughly estimated at one day per pound. Because we limit the total quantity of salt involved and dump the brine, it is safer to err on the longer time; without risking to over salt too much. Be aware that lean absorbs salt, fat does not and it is always the lean pork that gets too salty, you will have to learn to adjust for it.*
- Discarding of occurring brine, reduces the quantity of salt absorbed in the meat by about one third.
- *Up to this point, the procedure is the same in the next recipe for "speck Tirolese", only the salt quantity and possibly the spicing differs.*
- It is now time to cook the "jambon royal", in stock or oven with the option of smoking, if desired.
- Core temperature, 140° F, stock or room temperature 160-170° F with high humidity.
- Beware that a large piece will keep raising temperature at the core, after the removal from the oven or the stockpot.
- Don't let the core go much above 140° F to keep it moist and succulent.
- Refrigerate.
- If smoked the ham will keep for several weeks.

SPECK TIROLESE

Dry cured, smoked prosciutto from the Italian Tyrol.
We use the same preparation as for the "jambon royal", but the ingredients are adjusted to the requirements of a dry cured raw prosciutto like ham.

100 %	Pork boneless long leg

3.50 %   Salt and cure, saltpeter @ 0.03 %
0.50 %   Sugar
0.50 %   Pepper, rosemary, bay, juniper, coriander... as you like
           Non-acid starter culture

- *Follow the same procedure as for the "jambon royal" in the previous recipe, with the increased salt and different spices, till the completion of the equalization period.*
- For mostly esthetic reasons it is desirable to apply a thin casing or collagen membrane to the exposed meat surface, the skin surface does not require it; if the boning and trimming has been done carefully and the "speck" presents a clean and smooth surface, it can be further processed without it.
- The "speck" is either hung from the Achilles tendon, or laid down on a grate in the smoke house; it is also possible to insert the "speck" in a net or stockinette, if the muscles tend to separate, this can happen if the boning and trimming is not very accurate.
- Ferment and dry, the initial temperature can reach 80° F and last for a couple of days. Otherwise follow the salami procedure and refer to page 126.
- The smoking needs to be done in short periods of one hour or two in order to keep the temperature low, never above 80° F. smoking can be done while drying and if need be can be repeated later during aging.
- The drying will take about two month, aging beyond this time for about six month, will improve the texture and the flavor.
- Avoid excessive drying, the "speck" should shrink about 30 %, to age beyond that state it is important to keep it in a cool and humid place.
- **Aging care of the whole muscles,** see page 138.

BUENDNERSCHINKEN, CULATELLO

It is the prosciutto of the Swiss Grisons, the cut of meat is the same as the "culatello", but the production process simpler.

100 %	Pork leg skin on, boneless
3.50 %	Salt and cure preferably saltpeter @ 0.03 %
0.50 %	Sugar
0.20 %	White pepper ground
0.15 %	Nutmeg
0.15 %	Garlic powder
	Non-acid starter culture

- Use a regular cut bone-in skin-on pork leg (This cut is not demonstrated in the video or PowerPoint pictures). After removing the knuckle and the sirloin, with straight-down cuts, you will gain a compact ensemble formed of top round, bottom round, eye, and inner shank with the fat and skin attached, forming a fairly cubic volume.
- Start with removing the hip bone, be very careful not to cut into the bottom and eye at the hip extremity. Use the tip of the blade touching the bone to follow the pointed extremity attached into the muscles. Reducing the depth and size of the hole dug to remove the bone will allow for a final cut, right at the edge of the top.
- Remove the shank at the knee, follow the seam, do not cut into the inner shank.
- Starting at the knuckle, remove the whole knuckle muscle, exposing the femur.
- Remove the femur, being careful not to cut into and separate, topside and bottom round.
- Having the boneless ham flat down on the bottom round, with the topside up, cut down straight through the Bottom round at the hip bone edge of the topside and then, straight down alongside the canal left by the removal of the femur.
- Cut off the Achilles tendon at the extremity of the inner shank.
- Rub the salt and ingredients and lay down in curing tub, paying attention to always position the meat laying flat on the bottom round or inverted but never on the side, it would open and separate the two main muscles.
- Better to pack several pieces tightly together to help shape them.
- Keep in the cooler to cure and salt for at least a week, then turn each piece upside down, If there are several layers, the top is moved to the bottom in the next tub and the bottom layer gets on top, keep salting one more week.

- After the salting time, discard the brine and re-pack for an equal time of equalizing.
- Stuff the ham in a fitting casing. By now the ham should retain their desired shape.
- Hang the stuffed ham in a net.
- A simple stockinette can be used to simplify the process. Dip it in oil to avoid the sticking to the meat.
- Ferment, dry and age. Refer to FERMENTING, DRYING, AGING, page 126.
- **Aging care of the whole muscles,** see page 138.

PANCETTA ARROTOLATA

The ancient mode was to leave the skin on and age the "pancetta" for a very long time. Winter preserve were to last all year. Nowadays convenience demands the removal of the skin, replaced instead by a light casing.

100 %	Pork belly trimmed

1.50 %	Salt and cure, preferably saltpeter @ 0.03 %
0.50 %	Sugar or maple sugar
0.20 %	Black pepper ground
0.10 %	Cinnamon
0.10 %	Garlic powder
	Non-acid starter culture

- The belly can be trimmed, either after removal of the spareribs or after boning of the ribs and sternum (the last is of course meatier).
- The belly is cut as a rectangle, from the edge of the shoulder (note that most commercial bellies include a sliver of the shoulder meat, which would be better left there to be used for salami), along side the cut of the ribs, to that portion of the flank, which still has the hard fat outside layer (this will be 3" to 5" from the leg seam, cutting off the portion with the soft fat ("mouille"), then removing a strap along the opening of the belly to remove the eventual mammal tissues.
- A properly cut belly will show a thin seam of lean all along the rib-cut edge; it may be necessary to cut of a fat strap on that side too.
- It is important to remove all the soft internal fat and, where apparent, the silver membranes, in order to facilitate the binding.
- Refer to the demonstration in the video or the pictures in the PowerPoint.
- Rub the salt, cure, sugar and starter on the inside of the bellies,
- It is convenient to prepare several pieces at the same time. Stack them and lay them in a tub in the cooler.
- They will need 3-4 days to absorb the salt and cure. Don't expect much brine formation.
- Lay the cured belly on the fat side down, scrape all leftover cure from the inside.
- Reverse the belly and slice a wedge at 45°, going out and down, through skin and fat, without separating the wedge from the belly.
- Initiate the cut 2 " along the backside, (rib-side).
- Open out the wedge and turn the belly again.

- Sprinkle and rub he spices.
- Roll tightly, starting ad the belly's mid section edge.
- Secure the roll with 3-4 hard tied loops. Roll into collagen film or large casing.
- Tie very close and very hard, or use a strong elastic net.
- Hang for drying and aging.

Pancetta, being mostly fat sheltering lean seams needs more time to dry and age but is less demanding than salami.

Charcutier. Salumiere. Wurstmeister.

COPPA AND LONZO

Muscles from the dorsal spine separate in the Neck (CT Butt) and Loin.
They are processed in a similar way.

100 %   Pork loin or CT butt

    3.50 %   Salt and cure, preferably saltpeter @ 0.03 %
    0.50 %   Sugar
    0.20 %   Black pepper broken
    0.10 %   Garlic fresh
    0.10 %   Cinnamon or rosemary
            Non-acid starter culture

- The meat is trimmed into a compact form, avoiding loose edges.
- On the "coppa", in the middle of the neck edge a tough fat knot has to be trimmed.
- ¼" of fat covering is left in place on the "lonzo". On the lumbar side, remove the edge of the wide top sinew, (alongside the back mid-section).
- Put the "lonzo" and "coppa", together (since they tend to have a similar caliber) in a proper container, rub all the salt, sugar, ingredients and starter culture.
- Lay the meat down, possibly packed together in a single layer, cover with a lid.
- Set in the cooler for about 3-4 days, then, lightly massage with the brine and flip around, pouring the brine on top, salt for additional 3-4 days.
- *One can shorten or lengthen the time in function of the size and thickness of the pieces, the curing room temperature also plays a role).*
- The curing will firm up the meat and release brine, which can be discarded at this time. Let the "lonzo" and "coppa" equalize in the cooler for another equal period of time. *See note in "JAMBON ROYAL" about duration,*
- Apply a thin casing or collagen membrane to the meat surface or stuff into a large casing, like beef bung or de-nerved chitterling, poke to remove air and tie tightly.
- "Coppa" and "lonzo" are fermented at 70-80° F for 3-4 days, following, the salami procedure.
- The drying will last about 2-3 months, aging beyond this time will improve the texture and the flavor.
- Avoid excessive drying. Aging in a cooler works well.

Refer to FERMENTING, DRYING, AGING, page 126 and **Aging care of the whole muscles,** page 138.

THE AUTHOR

After 42 years in Europe and 33 in America, now over 70, François Vecchio has accumulated a unique experience as a butcher and sausage maker.

Born in Geneva, Switzerland in a family of butchers and farmers. Francois started his career with a butcher apprenticeship of three years, which immersed him into three cultures and traditions. It was French at home and in Paris, Italian with his cousins in Piemonte and, German or "Switzerdutch" in Switzerland and Germany.

Later he perfected his art of the "salumiere" during 10 years in Ticino, running the largest Swiss factory of salami, prosciutto and "mortadella".

After this first career in Europe, François married Christine Sueda a Japanese-American raised in Hawaii, The couple settled in California, where in the early 80's François launched an upscale line of "salumi", creating a new category of high quality meats from the West Coast, it was in Fresno, where he started a new enterprise.

After 10 years he moved on to San Francisco to work with one of the largest salami producers, Columbus. For another 15 years he kept pioneering quality over quantity, creating higher levels of "salumi". With Niman Ranch for three years, he worked closely with the Mid-West farmers, packers and processors, developing new products,

In Palmer, Alaska, during seven years, the couple took refuge from the bustle of the Bay to enjoy mountains and glaciers bigger than the Swiss with a bush plane; François held seminars for chefs at Mat-Valley Meat, the shop of his disciple Nate Burris.

Back in the 80's he did introduce the "salumi" to the specialty distributors of the major cities of America and he got to know many of the best in the trade and recently, as a consultant, he had the joy of participating and continues to help in many beginning of the new "salumieri".

François and Chris are now settled in Petaluma, California.

francoisvecchio.com
mailto:<franvec@gmail.com>

ADDENDA

Chronicle Books Video: < *http://www.youtube.com/watch?v=lCecAo_QmOc*>

Internet site: <*http://www.francoisvecchio.com*>

Facebook Group:
file://localhost/<http/::www.facebook.com:groups:353179794751745:>

http://www.francoisvecchio.com/breaking-and-trimming-the-whole-pig
Step by step pictures of the Break, Shoulder, Center, Leg boning, trimming of the whole pig are available to download or review as PowerPoint.

L'encyclopedie de la charcutcric

CHARCUTERIES, SALAISONS, PRODUITS TRAITEUR.
Dictionnaire encyclopedique
Soussana
Editions MAE-ERTI 2003
If you can read French, this is it! 1300 illustrated pages in two tomes

Erfolgreiche Rohwurstrezepturen, Bruhwurstrezepturen,

Kochwurstrezepturen, Oekologische Wurstrezepturen

Allgemeine Fleischer Zeitung AFZ
Herman Jakob
DEUTSCHER FACHVERLAG
http://www.dvf-fachbuch.de

Find a way to translate them, these are the best professional recipes and technical directions.

Salumeria & gastronomia della Swizzera Italiana

Bioethica Food Safety Engineering, Sagl.
Via Terzina 6, CH-6963 Lugano–Pregassona, Switzerland

Charcutier. Salumiere. Wurstmeister.

http://www.bioethica.org mailto:bioethica@bluewin.ch

Written by Aleardo Zaccheo, the perfect guide on how to operate in respect of the regulations and how to write HACCPs for the artisans of the Swiss and Italian Alps counties. Here is a very good incentive to learn Italian, or wait until we can translate it. In the meantime, contact Aleardo he speaks English fluently.

Counsel, troubleshooting, assistance

From the best experts I know:

Magi Sala

World consultant, with rare bio-chemical scientific foundation.
He runs Embutidos Turon SA.
Plandevall-Z I s/n
18179 Les Preses, Girona, Spain
mailto:<nepta@futurnet.es>
34-609-728-575 cell

Aleardo Zaccheo

Counsel in applied and environmental microbiology, specialist of high risk food items. Ticino, Switzerland.
Microbiologist and food engineer versed in the European and international rules and procedures.
Educated in USA, fluent English. Hands on experience, defends the tradition with an expert bio-chemist training.

BIOETHICA FOOD SAFETY ENGINEERING SAGL
Via Terzina 6
CH 6963 Lugano – Pregassona TI, Switzerland
<bioethica@bluewin.ch>
+41 91 600 2966 office
+41 91 600 2967 fax

Christopher Lee

Long time Alice Waters' chef, 15 years of "salumi" experience. Consulting in Europe and USA.

5724 Panama Ave.
Richmond, CA 94804-5520,
mailto:oldfashionedbutcher@gmail.com
510-407-3285 cell

Starter Cultures for Making Fermented Sausages

Starters production and selection, is a very sophisticated industry, requiring complex laboratories. Several sources are available. Amongst them Danisco Texel, Kerry and Hansen. For a long time I was getting excellent starters from BioAgro of Italy, but they gave up fighting the red tape of exporting here.

This is the best presentation of the category I have ever seen. I found it in the Internet. Hansen offer a whole array of starters, with different purposes in sight. It is a very complex subject. When you study it, remember that your goal is goodness in term of aspect, texture taste and flavor. High acidity and speed are not necessarily your friends.

Chr. Hansen Starter Cultures for Meat Products

Starter cultures ferment sausages, develop color and flavor and provide safety. The addition of any commercial culture to the sausage mix provides a safety hurdle, as those millions of freshly introduced bacteria start competing for food (moisture, oxygen, sugar, protein) with a small number residing in meat bacteria, preventing them from growing. It may be called a biological competition among bacteria. Bactoferm™ F-LC has the ability to control *Listeria monocytogenes* at the same time as it performs as a classic starter culture for fermented sausages.

Cultures can be classified into the following groups:
* lactic acid producing cultures (fermentation)
* color fixing and flavor forming cultures (color and flavor)
* surface coverage cultures (yeasts and molds)
* bio-protective cultures (producing bacteriocins). You may think of bacteriocins as some kind of antibiotics which kill unwanted bacteria. Some of the lactic acid cultures (*Pediococcus*) possess antimicrobial properties which are very effective in inhibiting not only *Staph.aureus* but also *Salmonella, Cl.botulinum* and other microorganisms, including yeasts.

The advantages of starter cultures are numerous:
- they are of known number and quality. This eliminates a lot of guessing as to whether there is enough bacteria inside meat to start fermentation or whether a strong curing color will be obtained.

- cultures are optimized for different temperature ranges that allow production of slow, medium or fast-fermented products. Traditionally produced sausages needed three (or more) months to make, starter cultures make this possible within weeks or even days.

- production of fermented sausages does not depend on "secrets" and a product of constant quality can be produced year round in any climatic zone as long as proper natural conditions or fermenting/drying chambers are available.

- they provide safety by competing for food with undesirable bacteria thus inhibiting their growth.

Although commercially grown starter cultures have been around since 1957, it is only recently that sausage equipment and supplies companies carry them in catalogs. As the hobbyist-sausage maker becomes more educated in finer aspects of the art of sausage making he will undoubtably start making more fermented sausages at home.

The most important microorganisms used in starter cultures are:

Microorganism	Family	Species	Use
Lactic Acid Bacteria	Lactobacillus	L.plantarum	acid production
		L.pentosum	acid production
		L.sakei	acid production
		L.curvatus	acid production
	Pediococcus	P.acidilactici	acid production/ (fast fermenting)
		P.pentosaceus	
Curing Bacteriz (color and flavor forming)	Kocuria (Micrococcus)	K.varians	color and flavor
	Staphylococcus	S.xylosus	color and flavor
		S.carnosus	color and flavor
Yeasts	Debaryomeces	D.hansenii	flavor
	Candida	C.famata	flavor

In addition to being very strong competitors for nutrients against pathogenic and spoilage bacteria, lactic acid bacteria are known to produce compounds named "bacteriocins" which can act against other microorganisms. *Pediococcus acidilactici* and *Lactobacillus curvatus* are known bacteriocins producers especially effective against the growth of *Listeria monocytogenes*.

Chr. Hansen starter cultures

There are many manufacturers of starter cultures that are used in Europe and in the USA and we are going to list products made by the Danish manufacturer "Chr. Hansen" as their products demonstrate superior quality and are easily obtained from American distributors of sausage making equipment and supplies. Even more the company offers wonderful technical support and we are deeply indebted to them for detailed specifications about their products.

5.3.1 Starter cultures for traditional fermented sausages

In the production of traditional style sausages, the fermentation profile must have a short lag phase in order to ensure the growth of the added starter culture at the expense of the unwanted bacteria. The acidification profile must be rather flat not going below pH 4.8-5.0 at any time. This will ensure that *Staphylococci* maintain their activity over a longer period of time; foremost their nitrate reductase and flavor forming activities.

Culture name	Bacteria included	Characteristics
T-RM-53	*Lactobacillus sakei, Staphylococcus carnosus*	Aromatic cultures with mild acidification
T-SP	*Pediococcus pentosaceus, Staphylococcus carnosus*	
T-SPX	*Pediococcus pentosaceus, Staphylococcus xylosus*	
T-D-66	*Lactobacillus plantarum, Staphylococcus carnosus*	Aromatic cultures with intermediate acidification
T-SC-150	*Lactobacillus sakei, Staphylococcus carnosus*	
T-SL	*Lactobacillus pentosus, Staphylococcus carnosus*	
The cultures listed above are specifically selected for traditional fermentation profiles applying fermentation temperatures not higher than 24° C (75° F).		

5.3.2 Starter cultures for fast fermented sausages

In the production of North European and US style sausages the fermentation profile must have a very short lag phase in order to rapidly on-set fermentation and exibit a fast drop in pH to below 5.3 within 30 hours as a minimum. This ensures an efficient inhibition of unwanted bacteria and an early on-set of fast drying. Total production time is typically less than 2 weeks.

Culture name	Bacteria included	Characteristics
F-RM-52	*Lactobacillus sakei, Staphylococcus carnosus*	Fast cultures targeted for fermentation temperatures 22-32° C (70-90° F)
F-RM-7	*Lactobacillus sakei, Staphylococcus carnosus, Staph.xylosus*	
F-SC-111	*Lactobacillus sakei, Staphylococcus carnosus*	
F-1	*Pediococcus pentosaceus, Staphylococcus xylosus*	
LP	*Pediococcus pentosaceus*	
LL-1	*Lactobacillus curvatus*	
CSL	*Lactobacillus curvatus, Micrococcaceae spp.*	
LL-2	*Lactobacillus curvatus*	
F-2	*Lactobacillus farciminis, Staph.carnosus, Staph.xylosus*	
LHP	*Pediococcus acililactici, Pediococcus pentosaceus*	Extra fast cultures targeted for fermentation temperatures 26-38° C, (80-100° F)
CSB	*Pediococcus acililactici, Micrococcaceae spp.*	Extra fast cultures targeted for fermentation temperatures 30-45° C, (86-115° F)
F-PA	*Pediococcus acililactici*	
HPS	*Pediococcus acililactici*	Very fast cultures targeted for fermentation temperatures 32-45° C, (90-115° F)

In the US style fast fermented sausages (35-45° C, 95-115° F, very fast pH drop, low final pH <4.8), Staphylococci are not added to the culture since they generally do not survive such fast pH lowering.

5.3.3 Starter cultures for enhancing flavor and nitrate reduction

Sausages fermented with a chemical acidifier such as Gdl or encapsulated acid instead of lactic acid bacteria generally require added *Staphylococci* or Micrococcaceae spp. to obtain acceptable flavor and color. Those single strain cultures are recommended in all sausage products in need of extra flavor or nitrate reductase activity. *S. carnosus* is more salt tolerant than *S. xylosus* and convey a more intense flavor in fast fermented products.

Culture name	Bacteria included	Characteristics
S-B-61	*Staphylococcus carnosus*	Flavor and color enhancing cultures
S-SX	*Staphylococcus xylosus*	
CS	Micrococcaceae spp.	

5.3.4 Starter cultures for surface coverage

Mold present on traditional sausages prevents mytoxin formation by wild molds. It allows for uniform drying and contributes positively towards flavor.

Culture name	Bacteria included	Characteristics
M-EK-72	*Penicillium nalgiovense*	White mold culture for surface treatment
M-EK-4	*Penicillium nalgiovense*	
M-EK-6	*Penicillium nalgiovense*	

M-EK-4 grows better at lower temperature and humidity and gives a marbled appearance. M-EK-6 is more dense and develops a more fluffy coverage. M-EK-72 gives a strong growth and high fluffy coverage when high humidity and temperature is available.

5.3.5 Starter cultures for bio-protection

Bactoferm™ F-LC is a patented culture blend capable of acidification as well as preventing growth of *Listeria*. The culture produces pediocin and bavaricin (kind of "antibiotics") and that keeps *Listeria monocytogenes* at safe levels. Low fermentation temperature (<25° C, 77° F) results in a traditional acidification profile whereas high fermentation temperature (35-45° C, 95-115° F) gives a US style product.

Culture name	Bacteria included	Characteristics
F-LC	*Staphylococcus xylosus, Pediococcus acidilactici, Lactobacillus curvatus*	Culture for acidification and prevention of Listeria

Meat culture with bioprotective properties for production of fermented sausages with short production type where a higher count of *L.monocytogenes* bacteria may be suspected. Bactoferm™ F-LC has the ability to control listeria at the same time as it performs as a classic starter culture for fermented sausages. *Use dextrose* as this culture ferments sugar slowly.

How to choose the correct culture

In order to choose the correct culture the following advise may be used as general guidelines:

1. What style of sausage is produced?

   o Traditional South and North European: choose cultures in paragraph 5.3.1.

   o North European fast fermented: choose cultures in paragraph 5.3.2.

   o US style: choose the *extra fast* and *very fast* cultures in paragraph 5.3.2.

2. A very short on-set of fermentation is needed

   o Choose a frozen culture instead of a freeze-dried culture.

   o Increase the amount of culture.

3. The salt-in-water percentage in the fresh mince is:

   o > 6% : avoid F-1, LP, T-SP and T-SPX.

4. The type of sugar is:

   o Glucose: all cultures will ferment.

   o Sucrose: avoid T-RM-53, T-SC-150, F-RM-52 and F-SC-111.

   These cultures contain *Lactobacillus sakei*, which does not ferment sugar well (see the table on page 43). This fact can be used to our advantage by adding sugars which will not be fermented, yet they will remain in the sausage contributing to a sweeter taste.

5. Nitrate is added as a color forming agent to the mince

    o   Choose cultures in paragraph 5.3.1. and 5.3.2 and adjust the process correspondingly to traditional/slow fermentation.
    o   Add extra *Staphylococci* or *Micrococcaceae spp.* from paragraph 5.3.1 to enhance nitrate reductase activity

6. A product with an intense flavor

    o   Choose traditional technology and cultures from paragraph 5.3.1
    o   Add extra *Staphylococci* or *Micrococcaceae spp.* from paragraph 5.3.3. to enhance flavor formation

Notes:

*   Technical information sheets provide the recommended temperatures for fermentation, however, bacteria will also ferment at lower temperatures, just more slowly. For example, the technical information sheet for T-SPX lists temperatures as 26-38° C, optimum being 32° C. T-SPX will ferment as well at 20-24° C which is not uncommon for "European" style sausages, and 48 hours or more is not atypical.

*   When freeze-dried cultures are used it is recommended to disperse them in water. Adding 25 grams of powdered culture to 200 kg (440 lbs) of meat makes uniform distribution quite challenging. That comes to about 1/2 teaspoon to 4.5 kg (10 lbs) of meat and the culture must be very uniformly dispersed otherwise defects will occur later on. For those reasons it is advisable, especially at home conditions, to mix 1/2 tsp of culture in 1/2 cup (150 ml) of distilled water and then pour it down all over the meat. Any tap water which is *chlorine free* will do, the problem is that different cities, or countries, sanitize water in different ways. Chlorine will kill bacteria and the process will suffer. For this reason it is recommended to use distilled water.

*   Mixing freeze-dried cultures with cold water for 15-30 minutes before use allows them to "wake up" and to react with meat and sugar faster when introduced during the mixing process.

*   Cultures distributed by Internet online companies are of the freeze dried type.

*   Once fast-fermented starter culture or Gdl has been added to the sausage mix, the mix should be filled into casings.

Troubleshooting Guide for Fermented Meats

Slow acidification
Frozen culture allowed to thaw and subsequently held to long before dispensing into meat.

Microorganisms exhaust nutrients in packet/can, reducing the pH resulting in a lower culture activity.

Environmental temperatures/humidities during fermentation inconsistent with recommended culture optimums.

Secondary growth in meat of contaminant microorganisms producing components that buffer pH drop.

Prolonged storage of the meat mixture at cold temperatures resulting in extended lag phase at the beginning of the fermentation cycle.

Cheese in product may contain phosphate that buffers pH drop; it also has a tendency to absorb moisture from surrounding meat.

Sausage entering the smokehouse/climate chamber colder than normal, for example by using very cold meat, which may prolong the lag phase of the starter culture.

Spice formulation adjustment that either decreases acid stimulation or inhibits the culture.

Excessive salt or cure addition that inhibit starter culture.

Culture contact directly with curing components may inactivate the starter culture.

High fat formulation that reduces the moisture content.

Large diameter product giving slower heat transfer.

Rapid moisture loss in product.

Insufficient carbohydrate source added to sausage mixture.

Fast acidification
Temperature/humidity is higher than normal.

Spice formulation adjustment that favors the culture.

Excessive water addition.

Product delayed prior to entering the smokehouse/climate chamber resulting in higher initial temperature.

Leaner product giving more moisture and lower salt-in-water.

Change of meat (from beef to pork) in recipe.

Smaller diameter product processed at high humidity.

Initial meat pH lower than normal.

Wrong combination of carbohydrate.

Too slow drying that allows longer acidification.

Charcutier. Salumiere. Wurstmeister.

Inconsistent acidification
Inadequate distribution, resulting in hot and cold spots in meat mixture.
Inadequate distribution of culture, salt, cure, spices, dextrose.
Diverse initial product temperature.
Stored product and directly processed product in same climate chamber; culture activated in stored product resulting in a faster fermentation.
Products with different spice formulations, meat components, casing diameters, pH or water/fat content.
Uneven temperature/humidity in the climate or fermentation chamber.
Uneven humidity in dry room causing different drying rates.
Too low acidification temperature.

No acidification
Culture not added.
Culture inactivated by direct contact with salt, cure components, or heavily chlorinated dilution water.
Non-compliance with recommended handling temperatures after thawing of frozen culture.
Insufficient carbohydrate added to sausage mixture.
Excessive salt content.
Antibacterial agents added to meat mixture (preservatives, chemical boiler treatments via steam, antibiotics in meat).
Culture exposed to high temperature during transportation or storage.

Too low final pH
Failure to monitor acidification.
Excessive carbohydrate source.
Insufficient heat processing to retard fermentation (cooking procedure).
See also Fast fermentation.

Insufficient moisture loss
Excessive humidity.
Excessive air speed and/or too low humidity sealing surface pores giving case hardening/dry rim. No moisture migration from product.
Excessive smoke initially that coagulates surface proteins retarding moisture migration.
Slow drying, too high pH.
No acidification.
Smearing (during grinding) preventing water loss.

Casing greasy due to fat melting commenced. Water outlet potential through casing greatly reduced.

Too much moisture loss
Excessive drying, too fast air velocity, too low humidity.
Too fast acidification.
Applying a too fast acidifier (wrong culture).

Souring of product, post-processing
Insufficient heat treatment to destroy microorganisms (cooking process) .
Residual carbohydrates in excess that permits secondary fermentation.
Excessive moisture and residual carbohydrates in non-cooked product.
Insufficient drying.
Temperature abuse post-packaging.

Off-flavor
Microbial contaminants either growing during fermentation or post-packaging.
Use of spoiled raw materials (meat).
Poor sanitation post-processing.
Chemical contaminant.

Discoloration/green or gray coloration.
No addition of staphylococci.
Oxidation of meat pigments via microbial contaminants, metal contaminants.
Exposure to sunlight.
High pH.
Excessive peroxide-forming bacteria.
Too low amounts of nitrate/nitrite added.
Too fast acidification.
Spoiled raw materials.
Chemical acidifier added.
Too low fermentation temperature.
Too much sorbate in the casing.
Growth of yeast on the surface.
Trace metals (unclean salts).
Grey/brown rim due to high smoking temperature.
Smearing preventing water loss giving spoiled (grey) center.
Excessive air speed and/or too low humidity, sealing surface pores giving case hardening/dry rim. No moisture migration from product giving grey center in sausage.

Mushy product
Over-working at mixer, chopper or grinder.
Excessive fat extension.
Insufficient salt level or no salt added.
Spoiled raw materials.
Proteolytic microbial contaminant.

Slimy, gassy-product
Yeast or heterofermentative lactic acid bacteria contamination in package post-processing.
Excessive moisture content.
Inadequate smoke concentration at product.

Greasing (fat melting)
Excessive heating rate (cooking process).
Excessive fermentation temperature.
Unstable meat mix, low-binding meats.
Overworking raw meat mixture.
This information is based on experiments made by Chr. Hansen GmbH using the Bactoferm (TM) starter culture. We hope that this information has succeeded in answering many of the troubleshooting questions that might arise.

35694513R00136

Made in the USA
Lexington, KY
20 September 2014